The Savoury Mushroom

Cooking with Wild and Cultivated Mushrooms

The Savoury Mushroom

Cooking with Wild and Cultivated Mushrooms

Bill Jones

RAINCOAST BOOKS

Vancouver

To my wife Lynn — thanks for keeping the weeds out of the garden

First published in 2000 by

Raincoast Books
9050 Shaughnessy Street
Vancouver, B.C.
V6P 6E5
(604) 323-7100

www.raincoast.com

1 2 3 4 5 6 7 8 9 10

CANADIAN CATALOGUING IN PUBLICATION DATA

Jones, W. A. (William Allen), 1959–
The savoury mushroom

Includes index.
ISBN 1-55192-300-9

1. Cookery (Mushrooms) 2. Mushrooms, Edible. I. Title.
TX804.J66 2000   641.6'58   C00-910684-7

Illustrations: Roy Schneider
Cover and text design: Gabi Proctor/DesignGeist
Cover image: ©2000 PhotoDisc, Inc.

Raincoast Books gratefully acknowledges the support of the Government of Canada, through the Book Publishing Industry Development Program, the Canada Council for the Arts and the Department of Canadian Heritage. We also acknowledge the assistance of the Province of British Columbia, through the British Columbia Arts Council.

Printed and bound in Canada

Contents

Acknowledgements vi

Introduction 1

Mushroom Advice 7

An Edible Wild Mushroom Primer 29

A Cultivated Mushroom Primer 49

⑥ RECIPES ⑥   Basic Mushroom Recipes 55

Appetizers 67

Soups 83

Salads 99

Side Dishes 115

Noodles and Pasta 131

Vegetarian Main Courses 145

Seafood Dishes 163

Meat and Poultry Dishes 177

Further Information 194

Index 196

Acknowledgements

I have been writing this book from the moment I went on my first mushroom forage. Along the way I've learned much from a number of kind souls who graciously shared their knowledge. Through it all, my wife Lynn has been a constant foraging partner, sharing with me the pleasure of the forest. Many of our fondest memories revolve around the hunt for fungi. Eternal thanks to my parents, Bill and Joan, for their love and kind nature. Cheers to Ken Wilkinson for the good advice, and good ales! The past and present members of the Vancouver Mycological Society have our undying gratitude for the generosity and hospitality they have given us.

A book like this is the product of many talented people: Carol Watterson and Brian Scrivener were there at the beginning. Then the ball was passed to Derek Fairbridge and the staff at Raincoast Books. The end result is a book that I hope will be of use to a wide range of people — from curious beginners to serious cooks. With any luck, all readers will find something they like, and maybe even add a new dish to their repertoire. Special thanks to Roy Schneider for the excellent illustrations that enliven the book; it was fascinating to see the technical wizardry needed to produce the vivid images. And last but not least, thank you to my many friends in the First Nations community; I feel deeply for the hardships you have endured, and I have a wonderful optimism for what the future will bring.

Mushrooms have been a catalyst for many friendships, adventures and more than a few wonderful meals. They have also led me to think long and hard on the ways we treat the land. I hope one day we will truly care for the forests and oceans, log and harvest in a sustainable manner and leave untapped expanses of old-growth timber for the next generation to wonder and marvel at. Trouble in the forest is trouble for all of us in the interconnected ecosystem we live in and we must not waste the precious resources with which we are blessed.

BILL JONES
COWICHAN VALLEY, B.C.
AUGUST 2000

Introduction

Mushrooms have always been alluring to me: part curiosity, part culinary desire and part danger. My earliest memory of this allure is of running through the forest behind my house with a pack of fellow 10-year-olds. We had built a small fort in a canopy of deadfall and were horrified to find that mushrooms had sprung up all over the floor of our playhouse. We wondered if they were poisonous. Perhaps warts might burst forth from anyone who touched them. Back in the 1960s we were raised on English children's stories with tales of talking rabbits, forest garden parties and mythical "wee folk" living in the hollow stalks of large mushrooms. Like brave young men we studied the mushrooms for hours, swapping stories of poisonings and suffering that wizards inflicted upon unsuspecting victims. Later in life, my study of mushrooms led me to discover another very different application of magic, which oddly enough also involved talking rabbits and forest garden parties.

It took time living in Europe for me to truly unlock the magic potential of mushrooms. While living in the South Downs of England, my wife Lynn and I were surprised to see fields covered with wild *Agaricus* mushrooms — the common white button variety. We asked around in the pub and were told that mushrooms grew everywhere. Nobody bothered to pick them. The possibility of death loomed prominently in their thoughts. We finally met a village elder who quite heartily recommended picking and eating the mushrooms. Armed with this knowledge we walked up to the hills behind our rented cottage and picked a basketful of perfect mushroom specimens. That evening we had pasta with plenty of mushrooms and garlic. We were astounded. The mushrooms had a depth of flavour unlike anything we had tasted before. Afterwards we basked in the glow of picking something from the wild and transforming it into pure satisfaction, an act of culinary magic.

After my time in the tranquil English pastures it was time to move on to the next level of my training: an apprenticeship at a two-star Michelin restaurant in Alsace, France. My time at La Cheneaudier was memorable on many levels, not the least being my introduction to serious mushroom foraging. In Europe you get accustomed to fantastic produce arriving at the back door of the restaurant kitchen: a cooler full of pheasant, a bushel of amazing tomatoes and, one day, a wicker basket brimming with wild mushrooms. I grilled the bearer about the location of the mushroom forest. My queries met with a shifty glance and a few muttered grunts. Once he left, my kitchen companions informed me that I had crossed the line — no one ever asked specifics! I was to learn the life of a European mushroom forager can be a secretive and lonely pursuit, as they trust no one. My sous-chef Terri was kind enough to show me the basics of where to look for mushrooms and what to harvest from local forests. I not only learned to avoid the local poisonous mushrooms, but also that they could be valuable indicators that edible mushrooms are fruiting nearby. Once I started looking for mushrooms, I was hooked. Each afternoon I would stroll out into the forest and walk the now familiar trails. When Lynn visited from London (and later Germany), we would take long and peaceful walks through the fall forest, picking many baskets of plump, perfect boletes.

As you can well imagine, the kitchen of one of the finest restaurants in France was well versed in the use of wild mushrooms. We used dried mushrooms for sauces and fresh mushrooms in every possible guise. Truffles crowned everything. One of my first challenges was to make the house signature terrine, composed of layers of truffles and foie gras (goose liver). I remember walking back to my room at the end of many long shifts, reeking of truffles. One rainy afternoon a Canadian friend visited me and watched me clean a new shipment of black truffles. I watched horrified as he took a golf ball-size truffle and popped the whole thing in his mouth. He laboured for a moment and swallowed the truffle with difficulty. I asked if he had gone insane, downing about $100 worth of truffle in one bite. "I thought it was a truffle, you know, the chocolate kind." I quickly ushered him out the side door of the kitchen, hoping he wouldn't breathe on the chef as we walked by.

Once initiated into the world of mushrooms, Lynn and I started to notice that mushrooms were everywhere: in markets, in the baskets of passing cyclists and in the menus of restaurants all over Europe. When it came time to leave Europe and return to Canadian soil, we thought that the joy of mushrooms would be gone from our lives. As luck would have it, I landed a job in Vancouver at the old Raintree Restaurant. I was thrilled to see large crates of mushrooms arriving with the daily produce: chanterelles, hedgehogs, yellow foots and cauliflower mushrooms. I now realized that mushrooms grew everywhere! Soon I was buying local guidebooks and studying pictures of familiar mushrooms along with a bewildering array of new ones.

Around this time, Lynn discovered the Vancouver Mycological Society. Here we found a group of like-minded individuals who love mushrooms and, unlike their wary European counterparts, delight in sharing their knowledge with others. We began a long and fruitful association that saw us create a mushroom cookbook for the society. Lynn edited and published the society's newsletter and I served a term on the Board of Directors. In return we received a thorough introduction to the world of fungi and a guided tour of the regional mushroom habitat.

Now I am a hopeless mushroom addict. I have mushroom posters, mushroom art, shelves of mushroom books, jars of dried mushrooms — and dreams of mushroom forages dancing in my head. With this book I hope to share a little of my joy of mushrooms as you use the recipes and explore the magic of mushrooms in your own kitchen.

Mushroom Advice

WHAT ARE MUSHROOMS?

Mushrooms are part of the fungi family of organisms. It is a curious and wonderful family with many strange and fascinating characteristics. We are just beginning to recognize the potential benefits of fungi, and much research is underway to find new medicinal and commercial uses for mushrooms. The name fungi is derived from the Latin term for sponge, which perfectly describes the structure of a mushroom: a fibrous structure waiting to absorb water. Mushrooms are distinguished from most plants by their lack of chlorophyll, a substance needed for plants to absorb energy and nutrients from the sun. Because of the lack of chlorophyll, some fungi have adapted to derive nutrients from the roots of trees; in exchange, they help to fix nutrients and elements from the soil, which are beneficial to the trees. Other mushrooms act as nature's recyclers by breaking down dead plant and animal matter into basic components. These organic components provide a good growing medium and help the soil retain moisture. Mushrooms are at home in pristine forests, grassy boulevards and on the sides of decaying buildings, anywhere that there are nutrients and water.

The main part of the mushroom organism consists of a fine network of rootlike structures called the mycelium. What we usually refer to as a "mushroom" is the fruiting body, which can be one of several blooms in a growing season. The reproductive technique for most mushrooms is a very efficient system of spores. A single mushroom can produce hundreds of thousands of spores. Mushrooms appear to suffer little from repeated harvesting of fruit. Even so, foraging for wild mushrooms demands respect. In order to ensure a sustainable production of mushrooms, we must practise restraint when picking, leaving behind enough mushrooms to repopulate the area. It is also considered bad form to pick tiny emerging mushrooms, as these will expand into full mushrooms if given the chance.

Habitat destruction is a much greater source concern the health of mushroom populations. The complex relationship between trees and fungi is seriously compromised when the forest above the mushrooms is clearcut or paved to make way for a new shopping mall. We are still learning a great deal about mushrooms and it is clear that they have much to offer. For example, scientists are using mushrooms as sensitive environmental damage indicators. The sponge-like fungi readily absorb pollutants like pesticides, herbicides, industrial chemicals and heavy minerals — even radioactive isotopes. Studies track the health of the environment by monitoring the pollutant levels in urban mushrooms. It is not safe to consume mushrooms from industrial areas, golf courses or roadsides, as they are likely contaminated by airborne pollutants.

Nourishment, pleasure and healing are just a few of the benefits that fungi bring to our table. Mushrooms have been used for thousands of years as a source of food and medicine, as well as for ritual purposes. The Chinese have embraced certain fungi as possessing properties beneficial to overall health and well-being. Recent studies have indicated that mushrooms may be beneficial in bolstering the immune system and helping the body eliminate toxins. Several mushrooms, such as the well-known shiitake, contain compounds that appear to lower blood cholesterol levels in addition to promoting the action of disease-fighting components of our immune systems. Current research focuses on common mushrooms such as the oyster, enoki, shiitake, shaggy mane and wood ear fungus — and is producing many encouraging results.

HOW TO USE THIS BOOK

Mushrooms have many similar characteristics. In general, you can substitute almost any edible mushroom in most of the recipes in this book. Sometimes one kind of mushroom is more suitable for a certain cooking technique, and it is highlighted in the ingredients list. Other recipes are more universal and call for "mushrooms" or "wild mushrooms," which leaves you free to use any available mushrooms. I find that the button mushroom, the commercially grown mushroom found in most grocery stores, will yield excellent results in most cases. Fortunately, life offers more than just vanilla ice cream. If you are adventurous, mushrooms that taste of spice, nuts, caramel, licorice, apricots and more are waiting to be discovered.

You might be surprised to learn that out of the huge array of mushrooms, only a few are deadly poisonous, and of the more than 100,000 types, only a tiny fraction is interesting from a culinary standpoint. Wise mushroom pickers learn to identify the poisonous mushrooms as well as the edible types. The safest way to enjoy the mushroom experience is to buy mushrooms from a reputable source. Public markets are an excellent place to shop for foraged mushrooms. With the rising popularity of mushrooms, many grocery stores now carry a wide selection. Specialty stores routinely carry five or six types of fresh mushrooms and up to seven or eight types of dried fungi. It shouldn't take much effort to find a suitable mushroom to make most recipes in this book. The Internet has become a prime resource for information through mycological Web sites, foraging chat rooms and suppliers of everything from dried mushrooms to mushroom growing kits (see recommended list page 194).

Dried mushrooms are a perfectly good substitute in many of the recipes. You might sacrifice a little texture (the mushrooms become chewy), but you gain a lot of intense mushroom flavour. In some cases the taste of dried mushrooms is superior to that of the fresh version. When substituting dried mushrooms in a recipe you usually need to chop them up into smaller pieces. Shiitake mushrooms are an exception: the texture of the re-hydrated whole mushroom is a sensual treat.

Please note that this is a cookbook and not a guidebook for foraging wild mushrooms. That task is better left to true mycologists, people who have written books with pictures and descriptions of the mushrooms along with tips on where to look. My favourite mushroom handbook is a gem titled *All That the Rain Promises and More*, by David Arora. It is compact and jammed with information and delightful stories on mushroom foraging. Mushrooms tend to vary in habitat and colouring as you move around the planet, so it's best to get a guidebook that pertains to your region. The wild mushroom season starts in the northern districts first, late in the summer, and moves southward as the season progresses. Many professional mushroom pickers on the West Coast start in Alaska in the summer and end up in Mexico in the winter.

At best recipes are only guidelines for good cooking. A good cookbook will introduce you to techniques that you can weave into your everyday cooking. Use the recipes to point you in the right direction, then use your own judgement when it comes to seasonings and cooking times. If you like your dishes spiced mildly, or blazing hot, feel free to make modifications. If onions make you shudder with revulsion, leave them out. If you hate cilantro, use parsley or basil in its place — no one will know. Above all, relax and have fun.

WILD MUSHROOM FORAGING

In 1996 Lynn and I compiled and self-published a cookbook as a fundraiser for the Vancouver Mycological Society. In that book, I wrote a description of a typical mushroom forage. The intent was to give the reader an armchair tour of a forest in the peak of mushroom season. It is a wet, damp and unforgiving environment that mentally and physically tests anyone who ventures into the wild forest. My account was meant to convey a healthy respect for the environment and to promote sustainable harvesting over greed. I've included that passage here to give you a little insight into fungi foraging.

On the Mushroom Trail — A Typical Foraging Expedition
(Excerpted from *The Vancouver Mycological Society Cookbook*, Bill and Lynn Jones, LynnWorks!, 1996.)

The excitement starts to build as we turn off the highway onto a dirt road heading up into the Coastal Range. Memories of previous visits and the edible treasure in the forest flash through my mind. The road turns in familiar patterns and landmarks to guide us to a dependable foraging area. Around a final, rocky turn in the road and then into a precarious parking spot tucked between the cutback and the well-travelled logging road. We stiffly get out of the car, stretch and prepare for a wet hike through the forest. Lots of wool, fleece and gortex are layered onto us. Having donned our protective armour, we plunge headlong into the bush. Without trails or maps to guide us, we head instinctively down the mossy slopes. At first, the forest is dark and foreboding. It feels too green and lush. Familiar sounds are replaced by whistling wind and creaking wood. After a while I get my bearings and begin to take a quick mental catalogue of the forest. The moss is saturated with moisture and makes a soft carpet for the forest floor. A tall and spiny stand of Devil's Club is noted and a potential route planned around it. Large strands of spider webs criss-cross the vegetation. Nearby a small animal scurries through a clump of salal berries. I imagine its cheeks puffed full of berries and seeds; successful in its foraging.

My eyes are growing accustomed to the filtered light. What was initially a chaotic collage of dark greens and browns gradually becomes subtle shades of tawny, chocolate, green, rusty reds and occasional flashes of white. Experienced mushroom foragers tune themselves into their environment. You look for subtle variations in familiar patterns, protruding colours, disturbed mats of leaves, anything that catches the darting search of your eyes. Something catches the corner of my eye — a flash of orange under a log. I stop and peer under the rotting deadfall. It's too orange to be a chanterelle, almost fluorescent. Brushing aside the debris, a large, wormy lobster mushroom is uncovered. A brightly coloured parasite has attacked a host mushroom. Scanning the area reveals several healthy Russula mushrooms, likely candidates for the host body. Feeling encouraged, I note that this is an indicator that choice edible mushrooms may be fruiting nearby.

We move through the wet underbrush. Each step dislodges moisture from the shrubs we brush aside. My clothes are becoming heavy with sweat and condensation. The hair under my baseball cap is quickly matting and compacting against my skull. Parting two young fir trees, I step over a log and onto a small bench running along the hillside. To the left there are slivers of dull orange. Stooping down, I pick up the shattered fragments of a chanterelle. Questions swirl around in my mind. Has someone been here before me? Are there any mushrooms left?

These unproductive thoughts are forced out of my consciousness as I return to the task at hand. From the past comes advice given to me by my first foraging partner, received while living as a student in France. "Humans are merely an advanced form of the truffle-hunting pig," he would gleefully tell me. Taking his counsel, I breathe deeply and search the air for the scent of mushrooms. Perhaps it is different on the West Coast. The smell of mushrooms seems to flood the entire region. It looks like I'll have to rely on my sense of sight.

Off to the right my wife shouts out our traditional signal, *"Champignon! Champignon!"* I resist the urge to run off in her direction and continue my slow, methodical search down the mossy bench. The forest is tranquil now, no stress, no traffic, only clean air pumped full of oxygen. I don't really care if I can't find mushrooms, even if dinner is already planned around them. Sure, I muse, who are you kidding! Another deep breath focuses my concentration. My foot twists suddenly to the side of a small orange clump, almost stepping on a beautiful, pale golden mushroom. Dropping into a squat, I carefully pluck the gem from the forest floor. It's a white chanterelle, a plump but anemic-looking relative of the common chanterelle. It's a choice and highly valued cooking mushroom. *"Champignon!"* I respectfully cry to my partner, who is crashing through the forest like an amorous grizzly.

Chanterelles tend to appear in groups, so I scour the area looking for the telltale flashes of orange. The dependable chanterelle seldom disappoints its admirers and I'm soon rewarded with about five pounds of fungi. The bench is long and continuous. I could keep foraging and double my harvest with little difficulty. In the back of my mind I think of the next people to walk in this area. Will they see our footprints and assume we've decimated the entire chanterelle population? I decide to stop picking and slowly, with an immense sense of communing with nature and my fellow mycologists, walk back toward Lynn. Pretty good picking, we both agree. "Let's head up to the higher elevations and quickly scout for boletes," I casually suggest. She looks momentarily puzzled, glances down at our bulging sacks of gold and shrugs her shoulders. "Sure, why not," she drawls. "There will always be other days." It wasn't until we drove back into the sprawling urban mass of Vancouver that I thought to myself — I certainly hope so.

Foraging Tips

The most critical time in the mushroom harvesting cycle occurs in the field when you first encounter the mushrooms. The time you take to properly clean and store the fungi will pay huge dividends in the kitchen. First and foremost, **respect the environment** around the fruiting bodies of mushrooms. Try to minimize your impact on the surroundings. This includes leaving behind large rotting (or worm-infested) fungi and any tiny emerging mushrooms. Mushrooms should be treated as a renewable resource. Try to disturb the forest floor as little as possible. Leave nothing human-made behind, except your footprints. When treated with respect, mushroom foraging locations will bear fruit for generations of mushroom pickers.

Carry a sharp knife and some sort of bag, basket or bucket to carry the harvest home. Mushrooms start to deteriorate the moment they are picked. A good circulation of air is necessary to help preserve the fungi until you can further process them. When collecting specimens for identification, some foragers wrap the individual mushrooms in paper (brown lunch bags work well). Plastic bags are not recommended, as they tend to make the mushrooms sweat. This will encourage the production of bacteria, which can develop into a health hazard. A good cotton grocery bag is an excellent choice for collecting. Pluck the mushrooms from the forest floor and cut off the root end. If the cut exposes worm trails (small brown channels and lines), cut off the wormy section or discard the mushroom in the woods. Some mycologists like to scatter these old mushrooms on the chance the spores will propagate. Place only clean mushrooms into your collecting bag.

It is not a good idea to mix mushroom types in one collecting bag. One poisonous variety can quickly spoil a harvest of mushrooms (and maybe the rest of your life!). Some mushrooms, like the shaggy mane, are highly perishable and easily crushed. They also have the annoying habit of self-digesting and can quickly turn into an inky mess unless handled delicately. Separate unknown mushrooms for later identification by wrapping them in paper or individual bags.

If you have done a good job in the field, the work at home should be fairly straightforward. Spread out some newspapers on a table and sort the mushrooms by type. Use a good guidebook and *positively identify* any mushroom that you plan to eat. Discard any questionable mushrooms or any that have deteriorated. If you are trying a new type, it is best to try only a small portion (after the mushroom has been positively identified). Wait 24–48 hours to see if any allergic or toxic symptoms develop. Common indicators of allergic reactions include an upset stomach and/or loss of muscular coordination. It is important to note that if a poisonous mushroom is ingested, symptoms may not be readily apparent for days. The deadliest types can induce organ failure, coma and death, so be very sure of your identification.

Once you have sorted your mushrooms, brushed off any obvious dirt, picked out the worms and insects and shaken out all the pine needles, you can now proceed to the next stage of preparation.

The best way to cook mushrooms is often the simplest. A quick sauté with garlic and olive oil is my personal favourite. Eating raw wild mushrooms is not recommended although you would have a hard time convincing many Italians of that. Mushrooms, like many foodstuffs, are prone to common bacteria such as salmonella, so care in handling is critical. In addition, some mushrooms contain toxins and undesirable enzymes that are rendered harmless by heating.

It is always safest to thoroughly cook your mushrooms. Certain mushrooms are incompatible with alcohol, and the interaction of the two may cause gastric upsets. Check with a recent guidebook to ascertain the latest details on mushrooms and their reactions. Remember that we all have widely varying metabolisms. A mushroom that is edible and delicious for one person may cause cramps and intestinal discomfort for another.

MUSHROOM POISONING

The number one rule to avoid poisoning is: **Eat only the wild mushrooms you**

FOUR MAIN CATEGORIES OF MUSHROOM POISONING
Imaginary:

Many reported mushroom poisonings are the product of anxiety attacks brought on by the person wondering if a poisonous mushroom has been ingested. These symptoms may include a tightening of the chest, light head, dizziness and nausea.

Allergic Reactions:

Mushrooms contain compounds and proteins that can affect our body's metabolism. Some mushrooms have a soothing and sedative effect, while others may cause trembling, nausea, headaches and hives. When trying a new mushroom, taste only a little bit and wait 15 minutes for a reaction. The symptoms of a reaction are generally mild and often the worst case scenario is a mild case of intestinal discomfort, which soon passes (no pun intended).

Hallucinogenic Reactions:

Certain mushrooms contain psychoactive chemicals (mainly Psilocybin) that trigger certain portions of the brain to misfire nerve receptors. This creates a somewhat

can identify with certainty! The number two rule is: **When in doubt, throw it out!**

In our mushroom society we have a wonderful annual event, "The Survivors Banquet." This tongue-in-cheek name is our way of poking fun at the poisonous potential of mushrooms. The vast majority of mushrooms are harmless, but several varieties (about 1–2%) have toxins that can shut down the functions of your kidney and liver and place you in a life-threatening coma. Death, although rare, does occur, particularly when large quantities of poisonous mushrooms are consumed.

There are thousands of mushrooms with complex and varying characteristics. Even experts in mycology need microscopes and DNA samples to

euphoric sensation and a highly altered sense of reality, which can result in hallucinations. Recovery from the toxin is usually rapid and the effects do not linger. These mushrooms have been used for thousands of years in a variety of religious and shamanic ceremonies. Local First Nations people used mushrooms during sacred vision quests in an attempt to help guide and solve the problems of the tribe. The abuse of hallucinogenic mushrooms is a major cause of mushroom poisoning, and often occurs because of misidentification, misuse or general stupidity.

Toxic Poisoning:

One mushroom in particular, the Panther Amanita (*Amanita pantherina*), is responsible for many poisoning incidents in our region. It gained a reputation as a magic mushroom but it also contains toxins that attack the liver and kidneys. The effects seem to be intensified with dried mushrooms. The Panther is a dangerous mushroom from the deadly Amanita family and should not be ingested under any circumstances. Other members include the Destroying Angels (*Amanita ocreata*) and the Death Caps (*Amanita phalloides*).

absolutely identify some mushroom types. If a common edible mushroom can be easily confused with a poisonous variety it is said to have a poisonous look-alike. When identifying edible mushrooms in the field, obtain a clear idea of the differing characteristics between the edible variety and the poisonous look-alike. One way to expand your ability to identify mushrooms is to buy a good guidebook (see page 195 for list). Colour, shape, gill and stem characteristics are some of the features that distinguish mushroom varieties. In the field a small pocket guide or mushroom flash cards can be carried to help with on-the-spot identification. Flash cards are a good way to quickly categorize mushrooms. The use of an identification key narrows down the choices for identification by using physical descriptions of the mushrooms. Joining a mycological society (or other natural history group) is a great way to meet like-minded people and to learn the way of the fungi.

What To Do if Mushroom Poisoning is Suspected

In the event of a poisoning, get medical help immediately and get the offending mushroom out of the system by vomiting as soon as possible. Many cities have poison control centres that carry information on mushroom toxins. It is now common for emergency centres to stock good guidebooks. If at all possible, bring in a specimen of the suspected mushroom to confirm the diagnosis and start the proper treatment. The main mushroom toxins attack the central nervous system and may result in headaches, vomiting and diarrhea.

Unfortunately, in the most dangerous cases no symptoms occur until most of the damage has been done. There are reports that some of the most deadly mushrooms were delicious and made a very satisfying meal (particularly the *Amanita* species). Two or three days later the patient may slip into a coma and never wake up. If you experience immediate symptoms you may be dealing with an allergic reaction or simple food poisoning. Young bodies can be particularly sensitive to such toxins. Be very sure of a mushroom before you feed it to a small child.

Avoid picking small white mushroom caps unless you are positive of the identification. At this stage it is difficult to distinguish many defining characteristics; edible and poisonous varieties can easily be misidentified. Avoid eating raw wild mushrooms and don't overeat — the mushrooms may cause havoc in your digestive system.

MUSHROOM CARE, HANDLING AND PRESERVATION

If you are lucky enough to discover a meadow filled with chanterelles or a backyard brimming with morels, you will want to preserve the bounty and enjoy your good fortune all year long. Certain mushrooms are best suited to certain preservation methods, and some are highly perishable and should be used as quickly as possible. There is wide variety in the structure, stability and chemical composition of fungi. Some mushrooms are very fragile and decompose quickly. Others contain toxic elements that render them inedible unless fully cooked. Still others are very watery in their natural state and the flavour actually improves with drying. The following chart highlights commonly available mushrooms and the preferred technique for preserving.

Wild and Cultivated Mushroom Preserving

Common Name	Latin Name	Cultivated	Wild	Dried	Canned	Frozen
Boletes (porcini)	*Boletus* Sp.		Excellent	Excellent	Good	Good
White Button	*Agaricus* Sp.	Excellent	V. Good	Good	OK	OK
Cauliflower Fungus	*Sparassis crispa*		Excellent	V. Good		Good
Chanterelles	*Cantharellus* Sp.		Excellent	OK		V.Good
Chicken Mushroom	*Laetiporus sulphureus*		OK	Poor		
Cremini (brown button)	*Agaricus* Sp.	Excellent	V. Good	Good		Good
Enoki	*Flammulina velutipes*	V. Good			OK	
Hedgehog	*Hydnum repandum*		V. Good	OK		Good
Horn of Plenty	*Craterellus cornucopiodes*	Excellent	Excellent		Good	
Lobster Mushroom	*Hypomyces lactifluorum*	V. Good	Good		Good	
Morels	*Morchella* Sp.	Rare	Excellent	Excellent		OK
Oyster Mushroom	*Pleurotus ostreatus*	Excellent	V. Good	OK	OK	OK
Pine Mushroom	*Tricholoma magnivelare*	Excellent	Good		Good	
Portobello	*Agaricus* Sp.	V.Good	Good	OK	OK	Good
Pom Pom (Bears Paw)	*Hericium abetis*	V.Good	V. Good	OK		
Shiitake	*Lentinus edodes*	Excellent		Excellent	Good	Good
Straw Mushroom	*Volvariella volvacea*	V. Good		OK	V. Good	
Truffles	*Tuber* Sp.	Rare	Excellent		OK	OK
White Cloud Fungus	*Auricularia* Sp.			V.Good		
Wood Ear Fungus	*Auricularia* Sp.	Excellent	Rare	Excellent		

Preserving Tips

In general, mushroom storage is all about the handling of moisture. If the mushrooms are wet, they will benefit from a few hours drying on a wire rack before cooking or processing. If the mushrooms appear dry (and are starting to crack), they will benefit from being stored covered with a damp cloth (or paper towel). Mushrooms should be well trimmed of all brown or decaying edges. Discard any mushrooms that appear slimy, exhibit mould, or have a "fishy" odour. These are all indications that the mushrooms are past their prime.

Do not soak or rinse mushrooms in excess water. Waterlogged mushrooms tend to decay rapidly and are also more difficult to sauté. The pan tends to fill up with moisture and the mushrooms stew instead of frying and building rich flavour. Clean mushrooms with a mushroom brush or damp towel, and remove any particles of dirt or forest debris. The cauliflower mushroom is one exception to this rule: it benefits from a deep and long soaking to rid it of trapped dirt and hidden insects.

For a large quantity of mushrooms, the best storage container is a plastic basket with full ventilation on all sides. Line the basket with paper towels and fill with cleaned mushrooms. Cover the top with a damp cloth (or paper towel) and keep refrigerated for up to 3 or 4 days. For small quantities, a paper bag is the best choice. The breathable material allows excess moisture to escape. Plastic bags cause the mushrooms to sweat, accelerating decay and providing a fertile ground for food poisoning toxins. Discard any mushrooms that shrivel or show obvious signs of decay.

Drying Mushrooms

If you are faced with a surplus of mushrooms, drying is an excellent and time-honoured way of preservation. Certain mushrooms dry extremely well, including:

- Chanterelles
- Hedgehog Mushrooms
- Boletes
- Horn of Plenty
- Button Mushrooms

- Morels
- Oyster Mushrooms
- Cauliflower Fungi
- Wood Ear Fungi
- Pine Mushrooms

A warm, dry area with plenty of ventilation is needed to properly dry fungi. If the area is too damp, harmful moulds may grow on the mushrooms and render them inedible. A good place for drying can be anything from a small commercial food dehydrator to an oven on low heat with the door slightly ajar, to a suspended rack over a hot-water heater. Another time-tested method is to string slices of fungi with a needle and thread and suspend anywhere near a heat source. Fireplaces are an ideal heat source and contribute a pleasant smoky flavour to the final product. Thin slices dry quickly but thicker slices often keep better over time.

Once you have dried the mushrooms, place them in zip-lock bags or glass jars with a tight-fitting lid. Moisture is the enemy of dried fungi; if present, it will cause the dried product to re-hydrate, and decomposition and mould growth will start.

Freezing Mushrooms

Freezing is another viable method of preserving mushrooms. In general the meaty and fibrous mushrooms are best suited to this technique, as their texture is not greatly affected. These include:

- Button Mushrooms
- Boletes
- Cauliflower Fungus
- Chanterelles
- Hedgehog Mushrooms
- Pine Mushrooms
- Saffron Milk Cap
- Horn of Plenty

Most edible mushrooms can be successfully frozen. Decomposition begins the moment they are harvested, but cooking and freezing will halt the process. Mushrooms can be preserved for 1–2 months if prepared and sealed properly. Many cooking techniques are suitable prior to freezing, including blanching in salted water, sautéing, roasting and grilling. In general, mushrooms must be fully cooked. Some varieties require repeated cooking with several changes of water. Others can be simply sautéed in butter or oil, seasoned, cooled and frozen in plastic containers or zip-lock bags. The firmer mushrooms (like the ones listed above)

MEADOW MUSHROOM
Agaricus campestris

give the best results as their tough structure survives the freezing process fairly intact. Do not freeze wet mushrooms as the water expands the cell structure and allows all the moisture to escape, causing them to collapse when thawed.

Label and date frozen mushrooms and use within two months of freezing for best results. If you want to store mushrooms for longer than two months, drying is the preferred technique.

COOKING TIPS

For all of the recipes in this book, a wide variety of mushroom types will give excellent results. Thick, dense mushrooms such as white button, cremini, portobello, porcini and chanterelle are interchangeable in almost all of the recipes. The recipes that call for specific varieties of mushrooms are designed to take advantage of the best qualities of that particular variety; however, you can substitute another variety and the result will still be very tasty. Your main concern will be the cooking properties of the mushroom. The water content of the mushroom is your best guide to selecting the cooking methods. Moist mushrooms benefit from being cooked over high heat to quickly expel the moisture and allow the mushrooms to brown and produce a rich flavour.

Pungent fungi such as pine mushrooms are too strongly flavoured (and expensive) to substitute pound for pound for regular mushrooms. A recipe that calls for a pound of button mushrooms might take only one small pine mushroom for flavour. Truffles also are not a good substitute in any of the mushroom recipes, but they make a wonderful addition to finish any of the dishes. However, the price and rarity of truffles make them a luxury that few of us can afford on a regular basis. Recently, truffle-infused oils have entered the market. A few drops of oil will infuse a dish with the pungent aroma of real truffles. Be careful not to use too much truffle oil, as it can quickly overpower a dish.

CHANTERELLES
Cantharellus cibarius

An Edible Wild Mushroom Primer

CHANTERELLES

France: *Chanterelle or Girolle*
Germany: *Pfifferlinge*

Italy: *Canterello*
Spain: *Rebozuelo*

The chanterelle family includes many strange and wonderfully coloured fungi, from pale creamy white to psychedelic shades of electric blue. Yellow chanterelles are abundant in Pacific Northwest forests. On many occasions we have encountered several hundred chanterelles within an hour or two hike. I have many fond memories of stumbling out of a heavily wooded forest onto a mossy meadow literally covered with plump chanterelles. Readily available in public markets and specialty stores, chanterelles are continually gaining wider exposure. Dry chanterelles are a step down in quality from fresh, as the drying process renders the mushroom very tough, with a slightly bitter and peppery taste. Frozen chanterelles are a good addition to soups and stews. Canned chanterelles are also widely available.

Chanterelle (yellow chanterelle) *Cantharellus cibarius*

Chanterelles are many people's favourite wild mushroom. They have a beautiful elegant form, are widely available and are fairly difficult to mistake for any other mushroom. This makes the chanterelle an ideal mushroom for the novice forager. The bright yellow-orange colour is often in striking contrast to the forest floor.

The chanterelle favours locations with a deep, lush carpet of moss along with a fairly mature canopy of trees. I've had great success in old-growth forests and mature second- and third-growth forests. Find one chanterelle and a careful search will usually turn up more hiding under the surrounding trees. In France, a small variety of the chanterelle is known as the *girolle*. In North America, you often find them dried or preserved in cans.

White Chanterelle *Cantharellus subalbidus*

In our area we are lucky to find this beefy cousin of the common chanterelle. The colour is pale white to cream when fresh. After picking, the mushrooms often discolour around the edges and the flesh appears to be slightly bruised in darker shades of orange. The stem of the white chanterelle is often much thicker than the other common varieties. The flesh is tender and mild — this is one of my favourite mushrooms for chowders and soups. The white chanterelle is often an indicator that conditions are favourable for the production of pine mushrooms.

One fine, rainy day in late October we were foraging in a mossy valley on Vancouver Island. We couldn't seem to find any edible mushrooms on a first casual survey of the area. I looked down at my feet and discovered I was standing on a beautiful white chanterelle, hidden under a carpet of oak leaves. We brushed back the leaves and found 20 or 30 plump white chanterelles staring back at us. We adjusted our eyes to look for the ruffled humps of leaves on the forest floor. Within minutes, my foraging partner and I each had our bags filled with perfect specimens.

Funnel Chanterelle (yellow foot, winter chanterelle)
Cantharellus infundibulformis
Often available at specialty shops, the funnel chanterelle is also a common component of dried-mushroom mixtures (particularly from France). This delicate mushroom quickly loses its shape after picking and can degenerate into a soggy, larva-infested mass if not stored properly. Wrap the mushrooms in plenty of paper towels and refrigerate in a container that provides lots of side ventilation. Drying the mushrooms actually helps to concentrate the flavour and results in a pleasing, firm texture.

Black Chanterelle *Craterellus cinereus*

A delicious and unusual mushroom with a bluish-grey to black underside that often appears dusted with a pale white bloom. The black chanterelle is delicious when sautéed in olive oil with minced garlic. This mushroom does tend to bleed a dark grey colour when cooked and will discolour pale dishes such as risotto and mashed potatoes. It grows in groups near mature hardwoods like oaks and poplars. In northern climates it is found in mature conifer forests with banks of mature moss.

Blue Chanterelle (blue cluster) *Polyozellus multiplex*

Not really blue, and not really a chanterelle, this striking mushroom is starting to show up with increasing frequency at local markets. It is categorized with the chanterelle family because of its superficial resemblance. The colour can vary from deep violet to bluish-black, but the blue colour tends to alter to grey-black after cooking. The flavour and texture are similar to the horn of plenty mushroom.

BOLETES

France: *Cèpe*   Italy: *Porcini*

Germany: *Steinpilz*   Spain: *Boleto comestible*

The bolete family is a large group of mushrooms. Underneath the cap of the mushroom you will find a sponge-like texture instead of the gills that many fungi have. The most famous member is the *Boletus edulis,* often called the king of mushrooms for its impressive size and flavour. The European boletes have a deeper, sweeter flavour than many of our North American varieties. This mushroom is one of the best for drying. The pungent earthy flavour is wonderful for making stocks, soups and mushroom infusions. Check boletes carefully for the presence of small worms, which like to burrow in through the stem and eat the flesh. An infected mushroom will appear soft and spongy — unappetizing for cooking or freezing but still suitable for drying. As the mushroom slices dehydrate, the worms will drop out: be careful to remove them before storing the dried slices.

ORANGE BIRCH BOLETE
Leccinum versipelle

Commercial bolete mixes often contain many bolete species; the more expensive contain only (or at least a high percentage of) *Boletus edulis.*

During my time in France I lived near wooded hills that were famous for their beautiful cèpes. We worked in the kitchen all day and took a two- or three-hour break in the afternoon. Each day I would hike the hills around the town and observe the daily changes on the forest floor. After a rain shower, it was amazing to see large boletes spring up from a previously barren forest floor. It really confirmed for me the relationship between mushrooms and moisture. The harder it rains, the more frequent (and larger) the mushrooms.

King Bolete (cèpe, porcini) *Boletus edulis*

The King Bolete is characterized by a distinctive swollen appearance. It is the most prized European mushroom and is known by several different names, most commonly as the porcini. As the King Bolete matures, its colour darkens and the spongy flesh becomes yellow-green and slimy. Commercial King Boletes are often cut in half to display the inner flesh. Top quality mushrooms display a firm, creamy texture free of discoloured worm trails. The King Bolete freezes well. Lightly sauté in garlic and olive oil or butter before cooling and transferring to a sealable container.

Other Edible Boletes (see below)
Boletus species, *Leccinum* species, *Suillus* species

Other Edible Boletes

- Yellow-fleshed Bolete *Boletus chrysenteron*
- Admirable Bolete *Boletus mirabilis*
- Smith's Bolete *Boletus smithii*
- Zellers Bolete *Boletus zelleri*
- Orange-Capped Bolete *Leccinum aurantiacum*
- Scaly-Stemmed Bolete *Leccinum scabrum*
- Slippery Jack *Suillus luteus*

- Short-Stemmed Slippery Jack *Suillus brevipes*
- Blue-Staining Bolete *Suillus caerulescens*
- Hollow-Stemmed Larch Bolete *Suillus cavipes*
- Dotted-Stalk Slippery Jack *Suillus granulatus*
- Lake's Bolete *Suillus lakei*
- Olive-Capped Bolete *Suillus subolivaceus*
- Woolly-Capped Bolete *Suillus tomentosus*

There are lots of boletes. Some are edible and delectable; others edible but inferior. A few are poisonous, but these are quite rare. Satan's bolete (*Boletus satanas*) is one of the few inedible types and does cause some trouble. It is a fleshy mushroom that exhibits a deep red spongy mass under the cap, which stains blue when pressed. The mushroom is very toxic when raw and is reputed to give great digestive distress to many people. In general the boletes are a relatively safe group to forage. The spongy pores under the cap (rather than gills) make the group easy to identify. The boletes are among the best mushrooms to dry, although some have a mildly bitter aftertaste.

MORELS

France: *Morille*   Italy: *Spugnola bruna*
Germany: *Speisemorchel*   Spain: *Colmenilla*

The morel is an unmistakable mushroom by virtue of its sponge-like head and pale, hollow body. Morels grow in older-growth forest, abandoned orchards, gardens, along roads and on sandy stream banks. The old saying that "morels grow anywhere but not everywhere" is a true description of the fickle nature of this fungi. Although generally associated with spring, morels can appear in any season.

   The morel family is an important source of income for commercial mushroom pickers. Morels are delicious fresh or dried and are greatly in demand by restaurant chefs. Morels tend to blend in with the surrounding landscape, and are well camouflaged. In an average spring, morels tend to appear soon after the crocus flowers bloom, when the land has just awakened from the throes of winter. The mushroom favours terrain where chaotic disturbances have occurred. Thousands of morels often sprout the year following a forest fire. I have watched patches of morels form near road cuts, excavations and fallen trees. Traumas that might disturb other organisms seem to accelerate the growth of morels.

Morels should always be eaten cooked. Raw mushrooms can cause allergic reactions in some people. A significant number of people exhibit dizziness and mild tremors when they combine morels and alcohol.

YELLOW MOREL
Morchella esculenta

Common Morel (grey morel)
Morchella esculenta
Usually found at lower elevations than other morels, the common morel fruits in late spring and favours a warm spell of weather after a particularly cold winter. One of the most commonly hunted mushrooms, it occurs in a wide variety of habitats. A comon variation, the Burnsite Morel (*Morchella atromentosa*), occurs up to two years after a forest fire, reproducing in prolific numbers.

Black morel *Morchella elata*

Commonly distributed over much of the planet, the black morel occurs in Europe, Asia, North and South America. The black varieties are particularly difficult to see in the forest. The head looks almost identical to a fallen pine cone. This mushroom occurs early in the spring and may be present well into summer. The black morel often occurs in high alpine meadows, fruiting much later than mushrooms at a lower altitude. Look for the black morel under conifers and shrub undergrowth.

White morel *Morchella deliciosa*

The white morel is probably the tastiest member of the family. It can sometimes grow to gigantic proportions and is one of the most prized mushrooms anywhere. Often fruiting under old fruit trees, the white morel may be spotted right up to Christmas in mild climates.

The Pacific Northwest is home to a giant morel species that can weigh up to several pounds. The old-growth forests of the region make an ideal place to absorb vast quantities of nutrients and moisture. In a quiet mountainside glade overlooking Howe Sound, I once found a huge white morel weighing over one pound. The morel was as big as a small roasting chicken — foreshadowing its role as stuffing the next day.

Half-free Morel *Morchella semilibera*

Often fruiting in sandy soil along streams and lakes, the sponge-like cap is partially connected near the top of the stalk (common morels are completely attached to the stalk of the fungi). The mushroom is a good edible but is fragile and prone to collapsing and crushing after picking. Handle it gently and you will be rewarded with a soft-textured mushroom with a delicate morel flavour.

TRUFFLES

France: *Truffe*   Italy: *Tartufo*

Germany: *Trüffel*   Spain: *Trufaldo*

Truffles are the culinary superstars of the mushroom world. They command fantastic prices and are regarded as one of the finer luxuries of life. The Perigord region of France and the Italian Piedmont are acknowledged as the home of the finest truffles. In fact truffles grow all over the world, and you are likely to see truffles from Oregon and China on sale in our local markets. The tuber grows underground and is usually found by virtue of its distinctive aroma. The scent of a ripe truffle is fairly close to the male sex pheromone for pigs, so naturally female pigs are trained to hunt for truffles.

A little truffle goes a very long way: fresh truffles are highly aromatic and potent. The truffle is normally shaved into paper-thin slices using a special mandoline. Store fresh truffles wrapped in paper towels, sealed in a covered container and refrigerated. The truffles will not last much longer than two weeks. Older truffles lose their scent quickly. The best way to store truffles is to clean them well and place them in a glass jar topped off with olive oil. The aromatic components are trapped by the oil, infusing it with a wonderful truffle flavour. Be sure to refrigerate the oil and use within one month. You can buy truffle paste and oil made from truffle trimmings, a good way to experience the flavour of truffles at a fraction of the cost. Use the oil in moderation as the pungent flavour will quickly overpower a dish. Also be aware that some commercial truffle oils are made from artificial flavours; more expensive oils are often worth the extra price.

There are many other truffles that are unusual, undiscovered or have limited culinary uses. Many are favoured by deer, rabbits and other forest creatures. The European truffles favour hardwood forests. In the Pacific Northwest they appear in a mix of forest, from stands of Garry oak to majestic old-growth rainforests.

Black (Perigord) Truffles *Tuber melanosporum*

A famous product of the broad oak forests of central and southern France, the black truffle is a gastronomic delight that has inspired chefs for centuries. Famous French philosopher Brillat-Savarin stated, "The black truffle could make women more tender, and men more agreeable." Pass the truffles! The true black truffle can cost in excess of $1,000 per pound and remains one of the most expensive food products available. Beware of cheap black truffles, as they may be mislabelled Chinese truffles, which pale in aroma and flavour compared with French truffles. The Perigord truffle has a blue-black exterior when fresh, fading to brown-black with age. Clean the truffle carefully with a soft brush to remove clay and dirt hiding in the soft knobby folds of the surface.

White (Piedmont) Truffle *Tuber magnatum*

Native to the foothills and mountains of northern Italy, the white truffle is considered the finest and most aromatic truffle. The tuber grows in symbiosis with oak, hazel, poplar and beech. The current market price for white truffles can be double the rate for Perigord truffles (partly due to the success in cultivating the Perigord truffle). The flesh is solid, light-coloured and very brittle. A fresh truffle can shatter if dropped on the floor. Large specimens, up to one pound, exist but most truffles are the size of large walnuts. The white truffle is slightly more perishable than its darker cousins. The flavour and aroma seem to diminish a week or two after harvest. The white truffle has a distinctive pepper edge and is often eaten raw. The skin is a dirty beige when fresh, turning darker brown with age. Clean the potato-like surface of the white truffle with a damp cloth.

Oregon White Truffle *Tuber gibbosum*

Recently, good quality white truffles have been found in Oregon and along the Pacific coast. The quality is not at par with Piedmont truffles, but the price is a little easier to swallow. These truffles like to associate with mature stands of Douglas fir and have been found all along the slopes of coastal mountain ranges.

Truffles are often found with the help of animals. When truffles are ripe, they give off an aroma that is highly stimulating to certain forest creatures. On a truffle hunt in southern France, I was introduced to the hunting of truffles with the help of the common fly. My guide was a seasoned veteran of the truffle hunt (I'm sure the only reason he took me out was to please his nephew, my friend) and was reassured by the knowledge that I would soon be flying

3,000 miles away from his truffle patch. As we walked through the open forest of oak and beech trees, my guide stopped us with a wave of his walking stick. On the dry ground ahead of him, a swarm of flies hovered near the base of a tall and stately oak. He dug down a few inches into the dry soil and uncovered an egg-size black truffle. Back at his small cabin we sat around an ancient wood stove and ate scrambled eggs tossed with French butter and truffles. It was a magical culinary moment, more perfect than the finest restaurant could produce.

PINE MUSHROOMS (matsutake)

France: *Champignon de pin*   Japan: *Matsutake*
Germany: *Kieferpilz*   Spain: *Seta del pino*

The pine mushroom is a highly valued mushroom that has been a member of the fungi elite in Asia for hundreds of years. The Pacific Northwest has been identified as a region with substantial numbers of pine mushrooms and a healthy and growing industry has grown up around it. The Japanese have exhibited an insatiable desire for pine mushrooms and have driven up the market to levels reaching several hundred dollars per pound for perfect pine mushroom buttons (grades 1–3). As the mushrooms mature, the size increases (grades 4–7) and the value decreases.

The pine mushroom has a firm, dense flesh and a spicy aroma that is reminiscent of cinnamon. The scent is a key factor in determining the identity of the pine mushroom. Look for the pine mushroom at higher altitudes in stands of mature Douglas fir. The mushroom starts fruiting in late August and continues until the first hard frosts. It is prone to worm infestations. A good mushroom will have a firm stalk and will be free of worm trails when cut open.

Pine mushrooms command a significant export price due to the strong demand from Asian markets such as Japan and Korea. Both countries produce their own crops, but when a weak season is encountered the demand and price will explode. The result has been a mushroom picking "gold rush" that has led to overcrowding, tension and occasionally violence in the picking regions. Often the pickers are people who live a nomadic existence, following the wild mushroom season as it moves down the coast.

Caution: A Poisonous Look-Alike
Smith's Amanita (*Amanita smithiana*) is very similar in appearance to pine mushrooms but the odour is not spicy. The cap will tend to rotate upward if the mushroom is placed on its side.

OTHER WILD FUNGI

Angel Wings *Pleurcybella porrigens*
These are medium-size, thin, fan-shaped mushrooms that grow abundantly on deadfall almost all year long. The delicate mushrooms are very fragile and can be easily crushed if you are not paying close attention to your cargo. Angel wings dry very well and have a subtle nutty flavour.

Wood Blewit *Clitocybe nuda* (a.k.a.: *Lepista nuda*)

This is a well-known edible, and quite deservedly so. It has a beautiful purple-blue colour, meaty consistency and good flavour. Some people think the taste is similar to pine mushrooms. Care should be taken when foraging this mushroom as it can be easily mistaken for several mushrooms in the Cortinarius family.

FIELD BLEWIT
Lepista saeva

Caution: Inedible Look-Alikes

Violet Cortinarius (*Cortinarius violaceus*) and **Lilac Conifer Cortinarius** (*Cortinarius traganus*). Several members of this family are toxic. The colour is highly variable.

Cauliflower Fungus (Ruffle Mushroom) *Sparassis crispa*

This is a unique large fungus that looks like a compact bunch of ribbons. Though not common, it is an excellent find since one mushroom may weigh several pounds. Soak the whole mushroom in a solution of cold water and salt to rid it of any insects. The aroma is very appealing and the clean meaty taste and crisp texture make it one of the best edible mushrooms. Look for this fungus growing at the base of rotting fir trees.

Chicken Mushroom *Laetiporus sulphureus*

This is a spectacular fungus that grows on tree stumps in early fall. Orange on top and sulphur-yellow underneath, it is unmistakable. Only the edges of new growth are tender enough to eat. The mature specimens acquire a strong, pungent aroma and a coarse woody texture, making them quite unacceptable for eating.

FAIRY RING
Marasmius oreades

Delicious Lactarius *Lactarius deliciosus*

These common forest mushrooms are easy to identify because they exude an orange-red juice (or latex) when cut. The outer flesh often tinges green when bruised. There is considerable difference of opinion about their culinary value. They are a common culinary delight in Russia, where they are preserved in salt and consumed with shots of vodka.

Fairy Ring Mushroom *Marasmius oreades*

The fairy ring is a common mushroom that is often seen growing in rings on lawns and meadows. The mushroom has a fine, distinctive taste, and it both dries and reconstitutes easily. Beware where you pick them. If the area has been sprayed with herbicides, pesticides or exhaust pollutants, the mushrooms will readily absorb toxins.

Caution: Don't eat mushrooms from roadsides or lawns sprayed with herbicides.

Field Mushrooms various *Agaricus* species

Similar to the store-bought common white button mushroom, wild field mushrooms are common and an excellent find. Be very careful to distinguish the mushrooms from the entire *Amanita* family. If there is any doubt, do not consume the mushrooms. Many poisonings are due to confusion over these two mushroom families. Make sure the gills are pink or chocolate, not white or yellow.

Caution: Poisonous Look-Alikes

Destroying Angels *(Amanita ocreata)* and Death Caps *(Amanita phalloides)* Young Amanita buttons look very similar to young Agaricus mushrooms.

Hedgehog Mushroom (Yellow Tooth Mushroom) *Hydnum repandum*

At first glance, this mushroom looks like a large chanterelle. The underside of the cap has a shredded appearance, like a tiny shag carpet. The flesh is firm and dense and is quite delicious in soups or stews.

Honey Mushroom *Armillaria mellea*

Often found in massive bunches on the trunks of dead trees. Many recent field guides include warnings about this well-known edible. The mushroom must be very well cooked. Toxins are present in the raw mushrooms but careful cooking and repeated changes of water render them safe. Even so, some people have mild allergic reactions to these mushrooms; caution is advised when consuming them for the first time.

Caution: Must be well cooked; may cause upset stomach in certain individuals.

Lobster Mushroom *Hypomyces lactiluorum*

A vivid red-orange mushroom, this fungi is a joint effort between a host mushroom (usually a Russula or Lactarius) and a parasite that attacks and transforms the host into an excellent edible mushroom. Warnings exist in the guidebooks that the host mushroom can be poisonous. Pickers should identify the mushrooms surrounding the lobster mushroom to identify the host. The lobster mushroom has a florescent orange crusty exterior and a firm and sweet flavour. Before its transformation, the host mushroom is usually a large white gilled mushroom. Lobster mushrooms are a well-loved treat, available in many markets along the West Coast.

Caution: Identify the host mushrooms surrounding lobster mushrooms.

Oyster Mushrooms *Pleurotus ostreatus*

A white to light grey, fan-shaped mushroom that grows on dead timber, usually alder, almost all year round. The mushroom grows in clumps and on deadfall near the banks of streams and rivers. The oyster mushroom is a good mushroom for the beginning forager because it is abundant and relatively safe to collect.

Shaggy Mane (Lawyer's Wig) *Coprinus comatus*

Nothing looks quite like these tall mushrooms with caps that never open up. Instead they auto-digest to release their spores, gradually disappearing into an inky mess. When young, they are good — very juicy and excellent in soups. This mushroom is extremely fragile and should not be stored for any significant length of time. If stored with other mushrooms, the shaggy mane tends to bleed black spores and discolour anything near it.

Caution: Poisonous Look-Alike

Alcohol Inky Cap (*Coprinus atramentarius*). Don't consume with alcohol.

Shaggy Lepiota *Macrolepiota rachodes*

This is another shaggy mushroom that should prove reasonably easy to identify, although it does have a green-spored look-alike that is poisonous. It is a large mushroom with a fine flavour, making it an excellent find. This fragile mushrooms should be handled with care and consumed soon after picking.

Caution: Poisonous Look-Alike

Deadly Lepiota (*Lepiota helveola*). The young buttons appear similar to Shaggy Lepiota. Look for mature specimens for identification.

Puffballs *Calvatia gigantea*

There are several species of puffball, all of them edible when young, while the contents are pure white. Giant puffballs can be sliced like a loaf of bread. When the puffball is ripe, the insides turn grey, then black. As the puffball dries out, it will emit a puff of spores if stepped on.

Caution: Toxic when mature; eat only pure white-centred puffballs.

SHAGGY MANE
Coprinus comatus

A Cultivated Mushroom Primer

White Buttons (Champignon de Paris) *Agaricus bisporus v. albidus*

Button mushrooms are underrated as a culinary ingredient. We take them for granted but they can always be counted on to add life to any dish. Commercial mushroom farming is now a big business and the industry has grown very efficient in the art and science of growing and shipping mushrooms. Buy mushrooms that are plump, white and free of surface blemishes. Buttons that have a thin white veil covering the gills will last longer than mushrooms with open gills. As the mushrooms mature, the gills darken from light pink to dark brown. A pronounced "fishy" smell will indicate that the mushrooms are overripe and should be discarded. Place buttons in a paper bag to allow maximum circulation of air and store in a refrigerator. Use within 2–3 days of purchase.

Brown Buttons (Cremini, Portobellini, Portobello)
Agaricus bisporus v. brunnescens
Common brown store-bought mushrooms are sold as young buttons under the name cremini. When allowed to mature to an open, mid-size mushroom, they are called portobellini. More commonly, the large, mature specimens are sold as portobello. Buy portobello mushrooms that have pink or brown gills. Overripe mushrooms have black gills, are strong-flavoured and have a mild "fishy" odour. In general, the texture of the brown button is superior to the common white button. The flesh is firm and the mushroom holds its dense shape when cooked. Store mushrooms in a paper bag in the refrigerator and use portobello mushrooms within 1–2 days of purchase.

Enoki Mushrooms (Golden Needle Mushrooms) *Flammulina velutipes*
Another culinary export from Asia, enoki are almost always sold in vacuum packages. These mushrooms are very fragile and highly perishable. The vacuum packaging helps prolong the shelf life and makes them stable for transport. The enoki is one of the few mushrooms eaten raw. Eat only recently opened packages. Cases of salmonella contamination have been reported in improperly stored enoki mushrooms. The flavour of the mushroom is mild

and nutty, making it a great last-minute addition to soups and stir-fries. Enoki mushrooms are becoming widely available and can often be found in Asian, specialty and health food stores.

Oyster Mushrooms (Abalone Mushroom) *Pleurotus ostreatus*

The current darling of the cultivated-mushroom scene, oyster mushrooms have seen many recent technological advances in production. The mushrooms are available in many colours, including white, yellow, brown and pink. Unfortunately the coloured versions fade to cream-grey when cooked. Oyster mushrooms are best when fresh and plump. As they age, the flesh tends to dry out and crack. Older specimens wilt and may have a pronounced "fishy" odour, so avoid these and buy only fresh, clean smelling mushrooms. Store the mushrooms in a paper bag or a mesh container, covered with a damp paper towel.

Shiitake Mushrooms (Chinese Mushroom, Black Mushroom)

Lentinus edodes

Shiitake mushrooms are native to China and have been cultivated for at least 1,000 years. A native of tropical environments, this mushroom needs heat, moisture and lots of nutrients to produce fruit. Commercially it is normally grown in bags of growing medium inoculated with shiitake spawn. Some small producers introduce shiitake spawn into hardwood logs (usually poplar logs). These produce dense, flavourful, premium mushrooms marketed as "Log Grown Shiitake." The stems of the shiitake are very woody and are often discarded. I like to save them in my freezer to add to a mushroom or vegetable stock. Dry shiitake mushrooms have a very intense flavour and are excellent in stews, and soups. Asian cultures place a premium on dry shiitakes with a cracked white cap, thought to be a sign of good energy or *chi*.

Straw Mushrooms *Volvariella volvacea*

A common mushroom in Chinese markets, the dense balls of straw mushrooms add texture and taste to soups, stews and stir-fries. Imported fresh straw mushrooms are sometimes available in our markets, however experimental farming is underway to establish straw mushrooms as a viable local crop. Dry straw mushrooms are occasionally available in Chinese markets, but they sometimes have a pronounced "funky" flavour and will be an acquired taste to Western palates.

Wood Ear Fungus (Tree Ear Fungus) *Auricularia polytricha* or *Auricularia auricula*

The wood ear fungus is a valued mushroom in Chinese cooking, and crunchy black slices are often found in hot and sour soup. The fungus has been used for centuries as a blood purifier and as a tonic for lung infections and stomach upsets. Usually available dried, it will keep indefinitely. A dry wood ear will expand to 3–4 times its size when soaked in water. Fresh wood ears are also occasionally available. The crunchy fungus can be added to salads, soups and stir-fries.

White Cloud Fungus (Silver Ear Fungus) *Tremella fuciformis*

This ivory-white fungus is closely related to the wood ear. Chinese chefs often use the white fungus in sweet dessert soups, and it is thought to enhance memory. The dried mushroom is soaked in water for one hour. The hard yellowish core should be removed before chopping up the fungus into bite-size pieces. The dried fungus will keep indefinitely.

Basic Mushroom Recipes

Dried Mushrooms 56

Mushroom Powder 57

Basic Mushroom Stock 58

Instant Mushroom Stock 59

Shiitake-Miso Stock 60

Mushroom Ginger Tea 61

Mushroom-Tomato Sauce 62

Sautéed Mushrooms 63

Steamed Mushrooms with Garlic-Herb Butter 64

Wine-Pickled Mushrooms 65

Dried Mushrooms

Makes 4 oz / 100 g

Drying mushrooms is an excellent way to preserve the harvest and spread the joy of mushrooms to all times of the year. The best dehydrated mushrooms are shiitakes, boletes, morels and horn of plenty mushrooms. The common button mushrooms make a tasty dried product. With varying degrees of success you can dry pine mushrooms, chanterelles, cauliflower fungi, oyster and lobster mushrooms. Drying seems to intensify the flavour of some mushrooms and enhances some of the therapeutic properties. Drying concentrates the harmful properties of some poisonous mushrooms. Careful and confident identification of mushrooms is essential when drying wild fungi.

| 2 lb | fresh mushrooms, thickly sliced | 1 kg |
| | salt and pepper to taste | |

Method 1

1. On a wire rack (cooling rack, metal grid or non-reactive screen) lay the mushrooms in a single layer. Season with salt and pepper and place rack near a heat source, such as a wood stove, hot-water heater or furnace. Cover with parchment to avoid dust and allow to dry for 2–3 days.

2. When brittle, place the mushrooms in a plastic bag or glass airtight container. Seal, label the contents, date and store in a dark cupboard.

Method 2

Oven: 200°F / 95°C

1. On a baking sheet lined with parchment paper, place the mushrooms in a single layer. Season with salt and pepper and place in a warm oven for 2 hours. Turn the temperature to the lowest setting (for gas stoves the pilot light is enough); place a wooden spoon in the door (to leave a small air space) and let the mushrooms sit overnight.

2. When brittle, place the mushrooms in a plastic bag or airtight glass container. Seal, label the contents and date and store in a dark cupboard. Will keep longer than 1 year if sealed tightly.

Mushroom Powder

Makes ½ cup / 125 mL

Mushroom powder quickly infuses the flavour of mushrooms into a sauce, baked goods or pasta. Use the powder to flavour coatings for fish, poultry and vegetables. Try pan-fried potatoes sprinkled with a little mushroom powder: the flavour is delicious. The mushrooms must be very dry to properly pulverize into a powder. If the environment is humid, dried mushrooms will re-hydrate and absorb moisture from the air. For this recipe, a piece of dried mushroom should be brittle enough to snap in two when bent. Dry the mushrooms in a low oven until they are crisp, and proceed with the recipe.

2 cups	dried mushrooms	500 mL

1. Place the dried mushrooms in a food processor (or mortar and pestle or spice grinder). Pulse until the mixture is a fine powder. Blend in batches if necessary. If the mushrooms are catching on the blade of the processor, they are too moist. Place in a warm oven until crisp and proceed.

2. Place ground mushroom mixture in a glass or plastic jar. Seal, label the contents, date and place in a dark cupboard. Will keep 6 months if sealed tightly.

Basic Mushroom Stock

Makes 4 quarts / 4 L

Stock is the foundation of good cooking. This recipe is a simple and quick version. Freeze the stock into 2 cup / 500 mL containers for sauces and into 4 cup / 1 L containers for soups and braising. Feel free to add chicken bones to the stock to add a smooth and rich flavour.

1 tbsp	vegetable oil	15 mL
1	onion, chopped	1
1 tbsp	sea salt	15 mL
1 tsp	cracked pepper	5 mL
2	carrots, chopped	2
1	celery stalk, chopped	1
2 tbsp	celery leaves, chopped	30 mL
1 lb	fresh mushrooms, chopped	450 g
1	head garlic, cut in half horizontally	1
1/4 cup	rosemary (or sage), minced	60 mL
4 quarts	cold water	4 L

1. In a stock pot over medium-high heat, heat oil for 30 seconds. Add onion, salt and pepper and cook until onions are soft and beginning to brown, about 3–4 minutes. Add carrots, celery stalk and leaves and mushrooms, sauté for 4–5 minutes. Add water, garlic, rosemary and bring to a boil. Reduce heat and simmer for 45 minutes. Remove from heat and allow to sit for 15 minutes.

2. Strain stock into a container and allow to cool to room temperature. The stock can be used immediately for cooking or transferred to sealable containers and frozen. Be sure to allow headroom in the containers as the liquid expands when frozen.

Instant Mushroom Stock

Makes 1 quart / 1 L

Sometimes you need cooking liquid in a hurry. Grinding mushrooms into a fine powder is like making instant coffee — just add boiling water. If you use whole mushroom slices, remove them from the broth after 15 minutes and finely chop. Return the mushrooms to the stock and allow to sit for an additional 5 minutes before using.

2 cups	boiling water	500 mL
2 tsp	mushroom powder (see page 57)	10 mL
	(or 4–5 dried mushroom slices)	
1 tsp	rosemary (or sage), minced	5 mL
1	green onion, sliced	1

1. In a heat-proof bowl or measuring cup, combine the water, mushrooms, rosemary and green onion. Stir well, set aside and allow to infuse for 15 minutes.

Shiitake-Miso Stock

Makes 1 quart / 1 L

Dried shiitake make a very rich and flavourful broth when soaked. You can remove the mushrooms from the stock at the end of the process and still have tasty braised mushrooms for use in other dishes. Try taking the cooked mushroom caps and tossing them with soy sauce, hot sauce, sesame oil and lemon juice — delicious. Miso is a highly nutritious substance made from fermented soybeans, rice and barley. Younger miso is sweeter, lighter, nuttier and less salty. Older miso is pungent and can be strongly salty. Feel free to add more miso to the broth if you like the flavour.

1 quart	cold water	1 L
10	small dried shiitake mushrooms	10
1 tbsp	dark soy sauce	15 mL
1 tbsp	miso	15 mL
4	thin slices fresh ginger	4
1	green onion, sliced	1

1. In a saucepan, combine the water, mushrooms, soy sauce, miso, ginger and green onion. Bring to a boil, reduce heat to low and simmer for 15 minutes. Remove from heat and allow to infuse for 15 minutes.

2. Remove the mushrooms from the stock, cut off the stems and return whole (or in slices) to the stock. Use immediately or strain and freeze.

The stock can be made into a quick vegetarian gravy by adding soy sauce, hot sauce and a thickener such as cornstarch, tapioca, potato, arrowroot or potato starch. Thin a spoonful of starch with cold water and add to the boiling liquid to thicken. Add enough soy sauce to yield a pleasing gravy colour.

The Savoury Mushroom

Mushroom Ginger Tea

Serves 2

Mushroom tea is a pleasing way to absorb the beneficial effects of mushrooms. You can add green tea to maximize the health benefits or simply use dried mushrooms. You may want to use a medicinal mushroom like Reishi (*Ganoderma lucidum*) in this tea. The Reishi mushroom is a key component of Chinese traditional medicine and is known as the "happy mushroom," "herb of longevity" and "food of the gods." The mushroom is a legendary immune system builder and is reputed to keep you calm, healthy and free of disease. If you find the taste a little bitter, add a teaspoon of honey to balance the flavour.

1 tbsp	dried mushrooms, chopped (shiitake, button, pine mushroom)	15 mL
1 tbsp	ginger, chopped	15 mL
1 tbsp	Chinese green tea	15 mL
2 cups	boiling water	500 mL

1. In a teapot, combine the mushrooms, ginger and tea. Pour over freshly boiled water. Cover and steep for 2–3 minutes. Pour into small cups and drink while hot. A second batch of water may be poured into the pot.

Mushroom-Tomato Sauce

Make 4 quarts / 4 L

Tomato sauce is the foundation for a lot of great food. Buy a basket of fresh tomatoes in season and stock your freezer with cooked sauce. Canned tomatoes seem to work very well in this sauce. If you search hard enough you can even find organic stewed tomatoes. I like the varieties that are stewed with basil leaves for a little extra flavour. The sauce should be adjusted to your personal taste for spiciness. Remember that it will get a little spicier as the dish sits.

I like to freeze the tomato sauce in zip-lock plastic bags. Lay the filled bags on a baking sheet and freeze into flat parcels. The sauce stores neatly in the freezer and the thin profile lets you defrost them quickly.

2 tbsp	olive oil	30 mL
2 cups	onions, minced	500 mL
3 tbsp	garlic, minced	45 mL
1 lb	mushrooms, diced	450 g
	(button, crimini, portobello, chanterelle)	
1 cup	celery, diced	250 mL
	salt and pepper to taste	
8 cups	stewed tomatoes, crushed	2 L
1/2 cup	tomato paste	125 mL
2 tbsp	basil, minced	30 mL
2 tbsp	marjoram, minced	30 mL
1 tbsp	brown sugar	15 mL
1 tbsp	hot sauce	15 mL

1. In a stock pot over medium-high heat, add oil and heat for 30 seconds. Add onion, garlic, mushrooms and celery. Season well with salt and pepper and cook until the vegetables appear dry and are beginning to stick to the bottom of the pot, about 5–6 minutes.

2. Add the crushed tomatoes, tomato paste, basil, marjoram and brown sugar. Stir well to mix and bring to a boil. Reduce heat and simmer for at least 20 minutes. Remove from heat and let cool. Can be used immediately or frozen for up to 1 month.

Sautéed Mushrooms

Serves 4

This is a general technique that works with almost any type of mushroom. You can also sprinkle a little ground mushroom powder on top of plain button mushrooms to infuse them with the flavour of exotic boletes or morels. The secret to great sautéed mushrooms is to evaporate the moisture as quickly as possible. You can easily squeeze the moisture from the mushrooms by rolling them up in a paper towel. Natural sugars in the mushrooms must be browned to release the full mushroom taste.

1 tbsp	olive oil	15 mL
1 tbsp	minced garlic	15 mL
2	shallots, minced	2
½ lb	sliced mushrooms	225 g
	(button, crimini, chanterelle, etc.)	
	salt and pepper to taste	
1 tbsp	fresh herbs, chopped	15 mL
	(chives, rosemary, sage, parsley, lovage)	

1. In a wok or large non-stick skillet over medium-high heat, heat oil for 45 seconds. Add garlic and shallots and sauté until the shallots soften, about 2–3 minutes. Add the mushrooms, season well with salt, pepper and herbs. Sauté until the mushrooms appear dry, about 5 minutes. Transfer to a serving platter.

Steamed Mushrooms with Garlic-Herb Butter

Serves 4–6

Steam cooking leaves the mushrooms with a spongy, soft texture and a velvet consistency. In place of the garlic butter, try a simple dressing of ginger, soy and sesame oil. Garnish with toasted sesame seeds and a sprinkling of sliced green onion.

2 tbsp	butter, melted	30 mL
1 tsp	garlic, minced	5 mL
1 tbsp	basil (chives or parsley), chopped	15 mL
1 tsp	cayenne pepper	5 mL
1 tbsp	lemon juice	15 mL
	salt and pepper to taste	
1 lb	mushrooms	450 g
	(button, morel, chanterelle, shiitake)	

1. In a small bowl, combine the butter, garlic, herbs, cayenne and lemon juice. Season well with salt and pepper and set aside until needed.

2. In a steaming rack, place the mushrooms and set over boiling water. Cover and steam for 5 minutes. Remove from heat and transfer to a serving bowl. Toss with the butter mixture and adjust seasoning if necessary.

Wine-Pickled Mushrooms

Serves 4–6

Pickling mushrooms is an excellent way of preserving them. The spicy bite of pickled mushrooms makes a great appetizer or side dish for rice. Use a non-corrosive pot (not aluminum or copper) for this dish or the acid will leach the sides of the pot and lend a metallic taste to the pickling solution.

1 cup	dry white wine	250 mL
2 cups	white wine vinegar	500 mL
1 tbsp	honey	15 mL
1	jalapeño pepper, split	1
2 tbsp	cilantro, chopped	30 mL
1 tbsp	ginger, minced	15 mL
1 tbsp	sea salt	15 mL
1 tbsp	whole allspice	15 mL
1	bay leaf	1
1 lb	whole mushrooms	450 g
	(chanterelle, button, oyster, portobello)	

1. In large non-reactive saucepan combine the wine, vinegar, honey, jalapeño, cilantro, ginger, salt, allspice and bay leaf. Bring to a boil, add mushrooms and return to the boil. Remove from heat and allow to cool to room temperature. Serve chilled or transfer to clean glass jars with tight-fitting lids and refrigerate for up to 1 month.

Appetizers

Grilled Oyster Mushroom Skewers 68

Mushroom and Shrimp Gyoza 69

Phyllo Spring Rolls Stuffed with Garlicky Mushrooms
and Vegetables 71

Wild Mushroom and Goat Cheese Pâté 73

Dungeness Crab and Enoki Mushroom Cakes 75

Chanterelle, Caramelized Onion and Asiago Quesadillas 77

Mushroom, Ham and Swiss Cheese Nachos 79

Pan-fried Tuna and Mushroom Bundles 80

Grilled Oyster Mushrooms Skewers

Serves 4–6

Oyster mushrooms are wonderful grilled. The delicate edges tend to char, adding a robust, nutty flavour. If you are not a fan of curry, simply substitute a spoonful of chopped garlic. The mushrooms cook very quickly and will wilt slightly when cooked through.

1/4 cup	vegetable oil	60 mL
1	small onion, finely diced	1
2 tbsp	curry paste	30 mL
1 lb	oyster mushrooms (48 pieces)	450 g
2 tbsp	basil, chopped	30 mL
12	wooden skewers, soaked in water	12
	salt and pepper to taste	

1. In a non-stick skillet, heat oil over medium-high heat for 30 seconds. Add onion and sauté for 2–3 minutes or until beginning to brown. Add curry paste and cook until fragrant. Transfer to a shallow dish and allow to cool.

2. On a flat work surface, lay 4 oyster mushrooms and run a skewer through the thick stems. Repeat with remaining mushrooms and skewers. Transfer to a shallow dish, coat with the curried onion mixture and sprinkle with basil. If the mixture is too dry, add a little additional oil to moisten. May be done 1–2 hours in advance.

3. On a hot grill, place mushroom skewers and grill until lightly charred and beginning to soften, about 2–3 minutes. Transfer to a serving platter and serve warm.

Mushroom and Shrimp Gyoza

Serves 4–6

Gyoza is the Japanese word for pan-fried dumplings. Also common in Chinese cooking, the dumplings can be stuffed with ground pork, chicken or vegetables. Dumpling (or wonton) wrappers are available in many Asian markets and large grocery stores. Available in round and square sheets, each package holds about 100. You can wrap excess wrappers in plastic film and re-freeze. The dumplings can also be frozen. To serve, pan-fry frozen dumplings over medium heat until browned and crispy, or add them to hot soup and cook until soft and warmed through, about 6–7 minutes using either method.

Dipping Sauce

1/4 cup	rice vinegar	60 mL
1 tbsp	soy sauce	15 mL
1 tbsp	fresh ginger, grated	15 mL
1 tsp	hot sauce	5 mL

Dumplings

1 cup	shiitake mushrooms, diced	250 mL
1 cup	fresh shrimp, peeled, chopped and de-veined	250 mL
1 tbsp	fresh ginger, minced	15 mL
1 cup	sui choy (Chinese cabbage), finely chopped	250 mL
1 tsp	sesame oil	5 mL
1 pkg	round wonton wrappers	1 pkg
1	egg, beaten (or water)	1
	vegetable oil for frying	

cont'd on page 70

1. In a small bowl, combine vinegar, soy sauce, ginger and hot sauce. Stir well to mix and set aside.

2. In a medium bowl, combine mushrooms, shrimp, ginger, sui choy and sesame oil. Stir well to coat and set aside.

3. On a work surface, lay out 4 wonton wrappers. Using a pastry brush, coat each with a light covering of egg wash. Place 1 tsp / 5 mL of filling in the centre of each wonton and fold to form a half moon. Be sure to keep edges free of filling to ensure a good seal. Press edges firmly to seal, making 3 or 4 small folds along the edge to make a pleated finish.

4. In a non-stick skillet, heat 2 tbsp / 30 mL oil over medium-high heat for 30 seconds. Cook dumplings, 8 at a time, until golden, 2–3 minutes per side. Transfer to a paper towel-covered plate. Transfer to serving plates or keep warm in an oven for up to 30 minutes. Serve warm with the dipping sauce.

Phyllo Spring Rolls Stuffed with Garlicky Mushrooms and Vegetables

Makes 16 rolls

Phyllo rolls make great party treats: golden, crispy and not greasy at all when wrapped up in lettuce leaves. Serve these as a main course with a side of noodles or rice and vegetables. As appetizers, serve with dipping sauce (page 69). Plan to make 2–3 rolls per person and roll into cigar-thick shapes for an elegant effect.

Oven: 400°F / 200°C

2 tbsp	olive oil	30 mL
2 tbsp	garlic, minced	30 mL
1	leek, washed and sliced thinly	1
2 cups	julienned mushrooms,	500 mL
	(shiitake, button, oyster, chanterelle, morel)	
1 cup	cabbage, shredded	250 mL
1 cup	bean sprouts	250 mL
2 tbsp	cilantro, chopped	30 mL
1 tbsp	hot sauce	15 mL
	salt and pepper to taste	
4 sheets	phyllo pastry	4 sheets
1/4 cup	melted butter (or vegetable oil spray)	60 mL
1 head	lettuce, washed and separated into leaves	1 head

cont'd on page 72

1. In a non-stick pan, heat oil over high heat for 30 seconds. Add garlic and leek and sauté for 2–3 minutes, or until soft. Add mushrooms and sauté for an additional 5 minutes, or until the mushrooms are soft and appear dry. Season well with salt and pepper. Add cabbage, sauté for 2–3 minutes or until warmed through. Transfer to a bowl and allow to cool slightly. Mix in bean sprouts, cilantro and hot sauce just before making the rolls.

2. On a flat work surface, lay one sheet of phyllo and brush surface evenly with butter. Top with a second sheet, brush with butter and cut the sheet into 4 4 in / 10 cm strips using a sharp knife or pizza wheel.

3. At one end of the phyllo strip, place a small line of filling across the bottom, about 2 tbsp / 30 mL. Roll pastry over to form a tight cylinder, fold in the sides to enclose the end of the roll and brush with a little butter. Continue rolling until near the end of the strip. Moisten with a little extra butter and roll to seal the pastry. Brush the entire pastry with butter and place in the refrigerator for at least 10 minutes. Repeat with remaining ingredients.

4. Place rolls on a baking sheet lined with parchment paper. Place in a hot oven and bake for 15 minutes or until golden brown and crispy. Gently transfer to a platter to cool slightly. Take a large leaf of lettuce and cut in half (slightly less than the width of the rolls). Wrap spring rolls with a lettuce strip and arrange (seam down) on the serving platter.

Wild Mushroom and Goat Cheese Pâté

Serves 6–8

This is a versatile pâté that works with a number of different herbs and mushrooms. Use your favourite herbs in combination with whatever mushrooms are available. Oyster mushrooms work particularly well; their flavour balances the tang of the goat cheese. I like using a fresh local goat cheese that has a clean, light flavour.

1 tbsp	butter	15 mL
2 tbsp	garlic, minced	30 mL
4	shallots, minced	4
2 cups	oyster mushrooms, chopped	500 mL
	(chanterelles, porcini, pine, morel, oyster)	
2 tbsp	fresh herbs, chopped	30 mL
	(thyme, sage, rosemary, parsley, cilantro or basil)	
	salt and pepper to taste	
½ lb	goat cheese, at room temperature	225 g

cont'd on page 74

1. In a non-stick pan, heat butter over medium-high heat for 30 seconds and add garlic, shallots and mushrooms. Season with salt and pepper and sauté until mushrooms are soft and appear dry, about 5 minutes. Remove from heat, stir in herbs, set aside and keep warm.

2. In a medium bowl, add goat cheese and soften with the back of a spatula. Add mushroom mixture and blend into the goat cheese. On a flat work surface, place a sheet of plastic wrap. Place cheese mixture on one side of the wrap and form a compact line. Fold over the plastic and roll into a smooth log, twisting the ends to seal the roll. Place in refrigerator and chill until firm. The log can be placed into a pâté mould (square, half round, triangle) to shape into other forms.

3. To serve, warm a sharp knife under hot running water and cut the log into thin slices. Serve on crouton rounds, crackers, or as topping for a salad of greens dressed with olive oil and balsamic vinegar.

Dungeness Crab and Enoki Mushroom Cakes

Serves 6–8

The foundation of these cakes is a mousse of white fish lightened with coconut milk. The Thai flavours complement the sweet flavour of the crab meat and the mushrooms add a wonderful texture to the mix. Dungeness crab is a West Coast variety. Buy fresh lump crab meat when possible and look for plump, white flesh. Check for shell and cartilage before using. You can also use frozen or canned crab for this recipe. Gently squeeze to remove excess moisture before using.

Ginger Mayonnaise

½ cup	mayonnaise	125 mL
2 tbsp	pickled ginger	30 mL
1 tsp	hot sauce	5 mL

Crab Cakes

½ lb	white fish, chopped (sole, snapper or halibut)	225 mL
½ cup	coconut milk	125 mL
	salt and pepper to taste	
½ lb	Dungeness crab meat, cleaned	225 g
2 tbsp	fresh basil, chopped	30 mL
2 tbsp	fresh mint, chopped	30 mL
1 tbsp	garlic, minced	15 mL
1 tbsp	ginger, minced	15 mL
1 tbsp	hot sauce	15 mL
1 cup	enoki mushrooms, chopped (1 package)	50 mL
4	green onions, sliced	4
1 cup	rice flour (or bread crumbs)	250 mL
2 tbsp	vegetable oil	30 mL
	additional enoki mushrooms for garnish	

cont'd on page 76

1. In a small bowl, combine mayonnaise, pickled ginger and hot sauce. Mix well and refrigerate until needed.

2. To a food processor, add fish and coconut milk. Season well with salt and pepper and pulse until a smooth paste is formed. In a mixing bowl, add fish paste, crab, basil, mint, garlic, ginger, hot sauce, enoki mushrooms and green onions. Mix well and place in refrigerator to chill for at least 10 minutes.

3. On a plate, place rice flour and season well with salt and pepper. Wash hands and scoop a little crab mixture (1/4 cup / 60 mL) into your palm. Roll mixture in your hands to form a smooth ball. Flatten between your palms to make a round patty; roll in the rice flour and set aside. Repeat with remaining mixture.

4. In a non-stick skillet, heat oil over medium-high heat for 30 seconds. Add crab cakes in small batches and cook until golden brown, about 2–3 minutes per side. Place in a warm oven and reserve until needed. Repeat with remaining cakes and serve with a small side of the ginger mayonnaise and a few fresh enoki mushrooms for garnish.

Chanterelle, Caramelized Onion and Asiago Quesadillas

Serves 6–8

Tortillas are widely available and are now offered in an interesting array of flavours such as whole wheat, tomato, red pepper and spinach. I've even run across curry and basil-flavoured products. Nothing, however, beats the plain tortilla for texture. Feel free to use your favourite cheese. The nutty flavour of Asiago works very well with the onions and chanterelle, as would Cheddar or Gruyère. The quesadilla is fine on its own or garnished with salsa and sour cream.

1 tbsp	olive oil (or butter)	15 mL
1	large onion, sliced	1
1 tbsp	garlic, minced	15 mL
	salt and pepper to taste	
1 tbsp	honey	15 mL
1/4 cup	white wine	60 mL
2 tbsp	fresh thyme, chopped	30 mL
1/2 lb	chanterelles, chopped	225 g
	(or button, shiitake, oyster or portobello)	
1 cup	Asiago cheese, shredded	250 mL
4	large tortillas	4
2 tbsp	vegetable oil, divided	30 mL
	additional chopped thyme for garnish	

cont'd on page 78

1. In a non-stick skillet, heat olive oil over medium-high heat for 30 seconds. Add onion, garlic and thyme. Season with salt and pepper and sauté 4–5 minutes, or until onions begin to brown. Add honey and toss to coat onions. Allow to brown evenly, then add wine to de-glaze the pan. Allow all moisture to evaporate. Add mushrooms and sauté until soft, about 5 minutes. Remove from heat and set aside.

2. On a flat work surface, place 2 tortillas and sprinkle half the mushroom mixture evenly over the surface of each. Divide cheese and sprinkle evenly over tortillas. Top each with a second tortilla.

3. In a non-stick skillet, heat half the oil over medium-high heat for 30 seconds. Carefully place the tortilla in the skillet. Reduce heat if the bottom browns too quickly. With a spatula, turn the tortilla and brown the second side. Place in a warm oven and repeat with the second quesadilla. To serve, cut into small wedges, garnish with chopped thyme and serve warm.

Mushroom, Ham and Swiss Cheese Nachos

Serves 6–8

These nachos elevate the perfect bar food to a level that would be at home at any swanky party. You can cook the mushrooms and onions ahead of time and just assemble and bake the nachos when you are ready to eat.

Oven: 400°F / 200°C

1 tbsp	olive oil	15 mL
1	onion, peeled and diced	1
	salt and pepper to taste	
4 cups	button mushrooms, chopped	1 L
1 lb	nacho chips (1 package)	450 g
½ cup	ham, diced	125 mL
1	red pepper, seeded and chopped	1
1	large tomato, diced	1
2 cups	Swiss cheese (Emmenthaler), grated	500 mL

1. In a non-stick skillet, heat olive oil over medium-high heat for 30 seconds. Add the onion; season with salt and pepper and sauté 2–3 minutes, or until the onions are translucent. Add the mushrooms and sauté until the mushrooms are browned and the pan appears dry. Allow to cool to handling temperature.

2. On a large baking sheet, distribute half the nacho chips evenly over the bottom. Sprinkle with half the mushroom mixture, ham, peppers, tomato and cheese. Repeat with a second layer, finishing with a top sprinkling of cheese.

3. Place sheet in the hot oven and bake for 10 minutes or until the cheese is bubbling and beginning to brown. Remove from oven and serve.

Pan-fried Tuna and Mushroom Bundles

Serves 4

Rice paper acts as a coating for these tasty fish sticks and helps to seal all of the moisture in. You can serve these bundles with either dipping sauce (page 69) or ginger mayonnaise (page 75). Keep the heat in the skillet under control. If the pan is too hot the rice paper will scorch before it can brown. Turn the heat down once the rice paper starts to sizzle.

½ lb	ahi tuna steaks	225 g
	(or salmon, halibut or snapper)	
1 tbsp	sweet soy (or teriyaki) sauce	15 mL
1 tsp	hot sauce	5 mL
1 tsp	cracked black pepper	5 mL
	hot water	
4	small rice paper discs	4
1 cup	shiitake mushrooms, sliced	250 mL
	(portobello, oyster or cremini)	
2 tbsp	cilantro, chopped	30 mL
1 tbsp	vegetable oil	15 mL
	salt and pepper to taste	
	fresh daikon or sunflower sprouts for garnish	

1. Cut the tuna steaks into thick rectangles (like a fish stick) and place on a plate. Drizzle with sweet soy, hot sauce and pepper. Toss well to coat and set aside.

2. To a large, shallow dish add hot water and slide in 1 rice paper disc. Allow to soften, about 30 seconds. Gently remove disc from water and place on a flat work surface. Lay marinated tuna across the bottom third of the rice paper. Top tuna evenly with 1/4 of the sliced mushrooms and sprinkle with cilantro. Fold the bottom of the rice paper over the filling, fold in the 2 sides and press to seal. Roll package in a tight cylinder and set aside. Repeat with remaining filling and rice paper.

3. In a non-stick skillet, heat oil over medium-high heat for 30 seconds and fry tuna rolls until rice paper is crisp and beginning to brown, about 2 minutes per side. Transfer to a plate lined with a paper towel and season well with salt and pepper. Transfer to serving plates and serve warm, drizzled with dipping sauce or mayonnaise, if desired, and garnish with fresh sprouts.

Soups

Chanterelle and Cauliflower Chowder 84

Asparagus Cream Soup with Sautéed Morels 85

French Onion and Cèpe Soup with Gruyère Croutons 86

Hot and Sour Mushroom Prawn Soup 88

Mushroom Minestrone 90

Purée of Leeks, Oyster Mushrooms and Cardamom 92

Barbequed Duck Wontons in Mushroom Broth 94

Lamb, Mushroom and Barley Broth 96

Chanterelle and Cauliflower Chowder

Serves 4–6

This chowder works well with many types of wild mushrooms. Choose mushrooms that have a dense texture and won't break down too much when cooked. The chowder freezes well and can be portioned into meal-size containers for future use. Potato starch is available in health and speciality food stores and is sometimes called potato flour.

2 tbsp	butter (or olive oil)	30 mL
1	onion, diced	1
2 tbsp	garlic, minced	30 mL
	salt and pepper to taste	
1 lb	chanterelles, diced	450 g
	(hedgehog, portobello, crimini, button)	
1 cup	potato, diced	250 mL
4 cups	cauliflower, coarsely chopped	1 L
1	celery stalk, diced	1
3 tbsp	flour (or potato starch)	45 mL
2 cups	mushroom or vegetable stock	500 mL
2 cups	milk	500 mL
1 tbsp	fresh rosemary, chopped	15 mL
1 tbsp	fresh sage, chopped	15 mL
	parsley for garnish, chopped	

1. In a stock pot, heat butter over high heat for 30 seconds. Add onion and garlic, season with salt and pepper and sauté for 3–4 minutes. Add the mushrooms and sauté until they are soft and appear dry. Reduce heat to medium and toss in potato, cauliflower and celery. Continue to cook for 5–6 minutes.

2. Sprinkle flour over top of vegetables and stir well to mix. Cook for 2–3 minutes and add stock, milk and herbs. Stir well to dissolve the flour. Bring the mixture to a boil. Reduce the heat and simmer for 10 minutes, or until the vegetables are tender. Ladle soup into soup bowls, garnish with parsley and serve immediately.

Asparagus Cream Soup with Sautéed Morels

Serves 4–6

Try to use local asparagus for this dish. Freshly picked stalks have a mild sweet flavour and are more tender than mature imported asparagus. Choose asparagus with plump stalks and firm and clean tips. Fresh morels are excellent in this dish. Dried morels (page 56) also work very well.

6 cups	mushroom or vegetable stock	1.5 L
1 lb	asparagus, trimmed and chopped	450 g
1/2 lb	spinach, washed and stemmed	225 g
1 cup	whipping cream	250 mL
	salt and pepper to taste	
2 tbsp	butter	30 mL
1/2 cup	shallots, sliced	125 mL
1 tbsp	garlic, minced	15 mL
1/2 lb	fresh morels, halved	225 g
	(button, crimini, oyster, portobello)	
	chives for garnish, chopped	

1. In a medium stock pot, combine the stock and chopped asparagus. Bring to a boil and cook asparagus for 7–8 minutes, or until soft. Add chopped spinach and cook for an additional 2 minutes. Transfer soup to a blender or food processor and purée in batches. Be sure to place a dish towel on top of the blender and press down firmly to avoid splashing hot liquid.

2. Strain soup through a coarse strainer or food mill (press solids with the back of a spoon or spatula) and return to stove. Add cream, season with salt and pepper and reserve until needed.

3. In a non-stick skillet, heat butter over medium-high heat for 45 seconds. Add butter and shallots, sauté for 2–3 minutes, or until shallots begin to brown. Add garlic and morels and sauté until mushrooms are soft and beginning to brown. Season well with salt and pepper. To serve, ladle soup into warmed soup bowls. Mound morels in the centre of the bowl and garnish with chopped chives. Serve warm.

French Onion and Cèpe Soup with Gruyère Croutons

Serves 4–6

Cèpes, also known as porcini or boletes, have a smooth and nutty flavour that really makes this soup special. A drop of sherry stirred in before serving adds richness to the broth. For best results use a good beef stock. Vegetarians can use a vegetable broth mixed with the soaking liquid from the dried mushrooms.

Broiler: High (when needed)

¼ cup	dried cèpe mushrooms	60 mL
	(horn of plenty, morel, shiitake)	
1 cup	boiling water	250 mL
1 tbsp	butter (or olive oil)	15 mL
2	medium onions, peeled and sliced	2
1 tbsp	garlic, minced	15 mL
	salt and pepper to taste	
1 cup	white wine	250 mL
4 cups	beef or mushroom stock	1 L
2 tbsp	fresh thyme, chopped, divided	30 mL
1 tbsp	fresh marjoram, chopped	15 mL
1 tbsp	sherry or port	15 mL
	croutons	
8	sourdough baguette slices	8
½ cup	Gruyère cheese, shredded	125 mL

1. In a small bowl, combine cèpes and boiling water. Set aside until water has cooled. Remove mushrooms from the broth and chop finely. Strain mushroom broth into a measuring cup, leaving any solids behind. Add chopped mushrooms to the liquid and set aside until needed.

2. In a medium stock pot, heat butter over high heat for 30 seconds. Add onions and garlic and season well with salt and pepper. Sauté for 4–5 minutes, or until onions are starting to brown and stick to the bottom. Add wine and reduce until almost all liquid is evaporated. Add stock and mushroom mixture and stir well to mix. Reduce heat and simmer for 10 minutes. Add 1 tbsp / 15 mL thyme, marjoram and sherry. Season well with salt and pepper and keep warm.

3. On a baking sheet, place the sourdough slices and top with remaining thyme and the cheese. Season each slice with a grind of fresh pepper and place under a hot broiler. Cook until cheese is melted and beginning to brown. To serve, ladle hot soup into serving bowls and top with croutons and serve immediately.

Hot and Sour Mushroom Prawn Soup

Serves 4–6

Shiitake mushrooms are excellent in a spicy broth. Look for soft tofu in most supermarkets. Try to find custard tofu (made with egg). Season the soup to your own tolerance for hot and spicy flavours. For a big boost in chili flavour, drizzle a little chili oil on top of the soup just before serving.

2	wood ear fungus pieces	2
1 cup	boiling water	250 mL
4 cups	chicken or vegetable stock	1 L
1 cup	tomato juice	250 mL
2 tbsp	garlic, minced	30 mL
1 cup	soft tofu, diced	250 mL
12	shiitake mushroom caps, sliced	12
1 cup	snow peas, julienned	250 mL
6	baby bok choy, halved	6
1	jalapeño pepper, seeded and chopped	1
1 tbsp	curry paste	15 mL
12	prawns, peeled and cleaned	12
2 tbsp	rice vinegar	30 mL
2	green onions, thinly sliced	2
2 tbsp	fresh cilantro (or basil), minced	30 mL
	salt and pepper to taste	
2 tbsp	cornstarch	30 mL
	(dissolved in equal amount of water)	
	cilantro (or basil) for garnish	

1. In a small bowl, combine wood ear fungus and boiling water. Set aside until water has cooled. Remove mushrooms from broth and chop into a fine julienne. Strain mushroom broth into a measuring cup, leaving behind any solids. Add sliced mushrooms to the liquid and set aside until needed.

2. In a medium stock pot over high heat, combine stock, tomato juice, garlic, tofu, mushrooms, snow peas, bok choy, jalapeño and curry. Bring to a boil, reduce to a simmer and add prawns. Cook until vegetables are tender and the prawns turn pink, about 5 minutes.

3. Season the soup with vinegar, green onion, cilantro, salt and pepper. Add wood ear fungus, return to a boil and whisk in cornstarch until the mixture thickens, about 1 minute. Serve hot, garnished with chopped cilantro or basil.

Mushroom Minestrone

Serves 4–6

A bowl of piping hot soup warms up body and soul. Use chicken stock for a sublime aroma and flavour. Cook the pasta until *al dente* and serve soon afterwards. If left in the soup, the pasta will absorb moisture and become mushy. You can make the soup in advance and add the cooked pasta just before re-heating and serving.

1 tbsp	olive oil	15 mL
1	onion, diced	1
2 tbsp	garlic, minced	30 mL
2 cups	mushrooms, diced	500 mL
	(porcini, portobello, crimini, button)	
1 cup	fennel, diced	250 mL
1	stalk celery, diced	1
4 cups	chicken or vegetable stock	1 L
2 cups	tomato juice	500 mL
1 cup	tomatoes, diced	250 mL
2 cups	kale, chopped	500 mL
1 cup	small shell pasta	250 mL
2 tbsp	fresh basil, minced	30 mL
1 tsp	hot sauce	5 mL
	salt and pepper to taste	
	olive oil for garnish	
	Parmesan cheese for garnish	

1. In a medium stock pot, heat olive oil over high heat for 30 seconds. Add onion and garlic and sauté for 2–3 minutes. Add mushrooms and sauté for an additional 5 minutes, or until mushrooms are soft. Add fennel and celery and sauté until the vegetables begin to stick to the bottom of the pot, about 3–4 minutes.

2. Add stock, tomato juice, tomato, kale and pasta. Bring to a boil, reduce heat and simmer for 8–10 minutes, or until pasta is cooked and vegetables are tender. Season with basil, hot sauce, salt and pepper.

3. To serve, ladle hot soup into bowls and garnish with a drizzle of olive oil and a sprinkling of freshly grated Parmesan cheese.

Purée of Leeks, Oyster Mushrooms and Cardamom

Serves 4–6

Enjoy the contrast between the smooth purée of the mushrooms and the crunch of the fried leeks. The soup can be made several days in advance. Add the cream just before serving. Freshly ground cardamom adds a pleasant camphor flavour that works well with the richness of cream.

1 tbsp	butter (or olive oil)	15 mL
4 cups	leeks, cleaned and sliced	1 L
1 tbsp	garlic, minced	15 mL
2 cups	oyster mushroom pieces	500 mL
	(or button, crimini, or cauliflower fungus)	
	salt and pepper to taste	
1 cup	white wine	250 mL
1 tsp	ground cardamon	5 mL
6 cups	chicken or vegetable stock	1.5 L
½ cup	whipping cream (or yogurt)	125 mL
	garnish	
1	leek, split, washed and julienned	1
1 cup	vegetable oil	250 mL

1. In a medium stock pot, heat butter over high heat for 30 seconds. Add sliced leeks and garlic and sauté for 2–3 minutes, until leeks are soft. Add mushrooms and season well with salt and pepper. Sauté for an additional 5 minutes, or until mushrooms are soft and appear dry. Add white wine and cook until the liquid is almost evaporated. Add chicken stock and bring to a boil. Reduce heat and simmer for 10 minutes, or until vegetables are very soft.

2. Transfer soup to a blender or food processor and purée in batches (be sure to place a dish towel on top of the blender and press down firmly to avoid splashing the hot liquid). Return to the pan, add cream and stir well to mix. Bring to a boil, check seasoning and adjust with salt and pepper. Reduce heat to a simmer and keep warm while you prepare the crispy leeks.

3. In a heavy-bottomed pot or wok, heat oil until hot (350°F / 180°C). Test temperature by adding a few strands of leek. The oil should bubble vigorously around the leek. Add leek to the pan and stir often until the leeks become crisp. When golden brown, remove from the oil and drain on a plate lined with a paper towel. Season well with salt and pepper. To serve, ladle soup into bowls, garnish with a mound of the crispy leeks and serve at once.

Cardamom is a tropical spice related to the ginger family. Its pungent flavour is often used in curries and is excellent in desserts. The spice is reputed to aid in digestion and is a home remedy for upset stomachs. Buy green-tinged whole pods, remove pod and grind to a powder for the best flavour.

Barbequed Duck Wontons in Mushroom Broth

Serves 4–6

If you're lucky enough to acquire a few pine mushrooms, this is a spectacular soup to serve at an elegant dinner party. You can use dried or fresh mushrooms and still have a great soup. For a vegetarian treat, use cooked minced mushrooms and finely diced tofu as a substitute for the duck.

Wonton

1	green onion, finely chopped	1
1 cup	barbequed duck meat, chopped	250 mL
2 tbsp	hoisin sauce	30 mL
	salt and pepper to taste	
1 pkg	wonton wrappers (50)	1 pkg
1	large egg, beaten	1

Broth

6 cups	chicken stock	1.5 L
1	small pine mushroom, thinly sliced (or 1 cup / 250 mL button, crimini or shiitake)	1
4	shallots, thinly sliced	4
2 slices	ginger	2 slices
2 tbsp	fresh cilantro (or basil), chopped	30 mL
1 cup	bean sprouts	250 mL

1. In a small bowl, combine green onion, duck and hoisin sauce. Season with salt and pepper, to taste, and set aside.

2. On a flat work surface, place 4 wonton wrappers. Brush the surface with egg mixture and place a small spoonful of filling in the middle. Fold the wonton to form a small triangle. Press with fingers to seal the edges. Take 1 corner of the folded triangle and press to the other corner to form a crescent. Set aside on a parchment-lined baking sheet and continue with the rest of the filling mixture. Refrigerate until ready to use. Wrap unused wontons in plastic wrap and freeze for future use.

3. In a medium pot, bring stock to a boil over high heat. Add mushrooms, shallots and ginger. Reduce heat and simmer for 5 minutes. Bring back to a boil and, while stirring, add wontons. Cook for 3–4 minutes, or until wontons float to the surface. Taste broth and season with salt and pepper if needed. To serve, ladle into bowls and garnish with cilantro and bean sprouts.

Lamb, Mushroom and Barley Broth

Serves 4–6

This dish takes a little bit of effort to roast the lamb shanks but the results are certainly worth it. The lamb, mushrooms and barley make a harmonious blend. The soup benefits from being prepared a day in advance and chilled overnight. Remove any hardened fat from the surface before re-heating and serving.

Oven: 325°F / 165°C

2	whole lamb shanks	2
1 tbsp	vegetable oil	15 mL
	salt and pepper to taste	
1 cup	carrots, peeled and diced	250 mL
1 cup	onion, peeled and diced	250 mL
1 cup	celery, diced	250 mL
1 head	garlic, peeled	1 head
1 tbsp	tomato paste	15 mL
2 sprigs	fresh rosemary	2 sprigs
1/4 cup	fresh whole sage leaves	60 mL
1 cup	red wine	250 mL
8 cups	beef or lamb stock	2 L
1 cup	pearl barley	1 cup
4 cups	mushrooms, diced	1 L
	(button, chanterelle, oyster or portobello)	

1. In a roasting pan, place lamb shanks and drizzle with oil. Season well with salt and pepper and place in a hot oven for 15 minutes. Add carrots, onions, celery, and garlic to the pan. Continue roasting for 20 minutes, or until vegetables and meat are browned. Add tomato paste, rosemary and sage. Roast for an additional 10 minutes. Remove from oven and allow to cool.

2. To a stock pot, transfer lamb and vegetables using a slotted spoon. Pour off any excess oil and place the roasting pan on top of the stove over high heat. Add wine and de-glaze the pan, scraping the bottom with a wooden spatula to dislodge browned bits. Pour contents into the pot and add stock, mushrooms and barley. Bring to a boil, reduce heat and simmer for 40 minutes, or until barley is tender. With a spoon, remove any foam that forms on top. Remove lamb from pot and allow to cool to handling temperature.

3. Add more stock or water if the soup appears too thick. Season well with salt and pepper. Remove meat from bones, dice into bite-size pieces and return to the soup. Reheat just to a boil, ladle into bowls and serve.

Salads

Spinach Salad with Mushrooms and Sweet Roasted Onions 100

Macaroni and Mushroom Salad with
Creamy Cucumber Dressing 102

Mushroom and Cabbage Coleslaw 103

Caesar Salad with Bacon-Roasted Chanterelles 104

Grilled Oyster Mushrooms on Mixed Greens with
Balsamic Vinaigrette 106

Warm Salad of Porcini and Barley with
Rosemary Vinaigrette 108

Japanese Rice Salad with Morels and Asparagus 110

Soy-Marinated Shiitake Mushroom and Rice Noodle Salad 112

Spinach Salad with Mushrooms and Sweet Roasted Onions

Serves 4

Warming the spinach gives the salad a soft, rich feel. To make a fluffier green salad, allow the mushrooms to cool slightly and toss in a salad bowl with chilled spinach leaves. The onions can be tossed with cayenne pepper for a spicy alternative. Stack the roasted onions on top of a mound of salad for a pleasing vertical presentation.

Oven: 325°F / 165°C

Roasted Onion Rings

1	white onion, cut in rings	1
2 tbsp	olive oil	30 mL
1 tbsp	honey	15 mL
	salt and pepper to taste	

Salad

2 tbsp	extra virgin olive oil	30 mL
1 tbsp	garlic, minced	15 mL
2 cups	mushrooms, sliced	500 mL
	(button, shiitake, morel, chanterelle, etc.)	
1 lb	spinach, stemmed, washed and dried	450 g
1	lemon, juice of	1
	freshly ground black pepper	

1. On a baking sheet lined with parchment paper, spread out onion rings and drizzle with olive oil and honey. Season well with salt and pepper and toss gently. Place in a hot oven and bake until browned and starting to crisp, about 30 minutes. Remove from oven and allow to cool slightly.

2. In a large non-stick skillet or wok, heat oil over medium-high heat for 45 seconds. Add garlic and mushrooms and sauté until mushrooms appear dry, about 5 minutes. Add the spinach to the pan and stir well until just wilted. Add the lemon juice and season well with salt and pepper.

3. To serve, immediately transfer salad to 4 serving plates and stack the roasted onions on top. Garnish with a grinding of fresh black pepper and serve immediately.

Macaroni and Mushroom Salad with Creamy Cucumber Dressing

Serves 4

This is a new spin on an old summer standby. Portobello mushrooms are the easiest to work with. One large mushroom will yield about 2 cups of diced mushrooms. The hot sauce adds a little zip to the salad but the dish also works well simply seasoned with salt and pepper. If you are a fan of pickled cucumbers (dill or sweet), add a few chopped pickles on top for a garnish.

2 cups	small elbow macaroni	500 mL
4 cups	mushrooms, cubed	1 L
	(portobello, white or brown button)	
1 tbsp	olive oil	15 mL
1/4 cup	mayonnaise	60 mL
1/4 cup	sour cream	60 mL
1 tsp	hot sauce	5 mL
2 tbsp	green pickle relish	30 mL
1	lemon, juice and zest of	1
	salt and pepper to taste	
1	English cucumber, cubed	1
2	green onions, sliced	2

1. In a medium stock pot filled with boiling salted water, add the macaroni and cook for 5 minutes. Add the mushrooms and cook for an additional 2–3 minutes or until the pasta is *al dente*. Drain and toss with the olive oil. Set aside and allow to cool.

2. In a large bowl, combine the mayonnaise, sour cream, hot sauce, relish, lemon juice and zest. Stir well to mix and toss in the macaroni, mushrooms, cucumber and green onions. Serve family style in a large bowl or in individual portions at a casual outdoor meal.

Mushroom and Cabbage Coleslaw

Serves 4-6

Sometimes I get a craving for crunchy cabbage, usually in the dead of winter when the last garden-fresh salad green is a distant memory. The mushrooms and onions are blanched to give them a soft texture and take away a little of the bite from the onions. As the dish sits, water will be drawn from the cabbage. Use a pair of tongs to lift up the slaw and shake free the excess moisture before serving.

3 tbsp	mustard	45 mL
1 cup	sour cream (or yogurt)	250 mL
2 tbsp	fresh chives, minced	30 mL
2 tbsp	white wine vinegar	30 mL
1 tsp	cayenne pepper	5 mL
	salt and pepper to taste	
1	onion, sliced	1
2 cups	mushrooms, julienned	500 mL
	(portobello, white or brown button, oyster)	
6 cups	green cabbage, shredded	1.5 L
2 cups	carrots, coarsely grated	500 mL
3 tbsp	parsley, chopped	45 mL

1. In a large bowl, combine the mustard, sour cream, chives, parsley, vinegar, cayenne, salt and pepper. Mix well and set aside.

2. To a stock pot filled with boiling salted water, add onions and mushrooms. Cook for 2–3 minutes and drain into a colander.

3. When vegetables have cooled, add them to the bowl along with the cabbage and carrots. Adjust seasoning with salt and pepper, toss well to mix and chill until cold. Serve family style or as a side vegetable.

Caesar Salad with Bacon-Roasted Chanterelles

Serves 4

Roasting the mushrooms with the bacon provides a tasty (albeit somewhat decadent) accent for the crisp romaine leaves. You can omit the bacon and simply toss the mushrooms in olive oil for a reasonable substitute. For a more exotic-looking salad, look for red romaine leaves in your local market.

Oven: 350°F / 180°C

Dressing

1	garlic clove, finely minced	1
1 tsp	Worcestershire sauce	5 mL
1 tsp	hot sauce	5 mL
1 tbsp	oyster sauce (or minced anchovies)	15 mL
1 tbsp	Dijon mustard	15 mL
1 tbsp	mayonnaise (or sour cream)	15 mL
1	lemon, juice and zest	1
¼ cup	extra virgin olive oil	60 mL
	salt and pepper to taste	

Salad

1 lb	chanterelles, cleaned and coarsely chopped (bolete, portobello or button)	450 g
2 slices	bacon, minced	2 slices
1 tbsp	garlic, minced	15 mL
½ cup	shallots, sliced	125 mL
1 head	romaine lettuce (green or red), washed	1 head
2 tbsp	Parmesan cheese, freshly grated	30 mL
	Parmesan for garnish, shaved	

1. In a small bowl, combine garlic, Worcestershire sauce, hot sauce, oyster sauce, mustard, mayonnaise, lemon juice and zest. Whisk to mix and add oil in a slow and steady stream until incorporated. Season well with salt and pepper and set aside until needed.

2. On a baking sheet, combine chanterelles, bacon, garlic and shallots. Season well with salt and pepper and place in the hot oven. Roast for 25–30 minutes, stirring occasionally with a wooden spoon until browned (and bacon is crisp). Remove to a paper towel-lined plate to cool and absorb excess fat.

3. In a salad bowl, rip the romaine into bite-size chunks (leave tender young leaves whole) and top with the chanterelle mixture. Add dressing and grated Parmesan cheese and toss well to mix. Transfer to salad plates and garnish with shaved Parmesan.

Grilled Oyster Mushrooms on Mixed Greens with Balsamic Vinaigrette

Serves 4–6

The slight charring of the mushrooms works well with the sweetness of the balsamic vinegar. You can buy a pre-made salad mix like mesclun and have good results. Make sure the greens are crisp or refresh in a bath of cold water. A salad spinner works well to rid the leaves of excess moisture. Place in the fridge for 5–10 minutes after washing, and even tired greens will be revitalized.

Grill: Hot

Mushrooms

1 tbsp	fresh ginger, minced	15 mL
1 tsp	sesame oil	5 mL
1 tsp	hot sauce	5 mL
2 tbsp	extra virgin olive oil	30 mL
1 lb	oyster mushroom pieces	450 g
	salt and pepper to taste	

Salad

6 cups	mixed salad greens, washed	1.5 L
	(lettuce, mustards, radicchio, arugula, etc.)	
2 tbsp	balsamic vinegar	30 mL
2 tbsp	light soy sauce	30 mL
2 tbsp	extra virgin olive oil	30 mL
	toasted sesame seeds for garnish	
	nori (sushi seaweed), shredded for garnish	

1. In a bowl, combine ginger, sesame oil, hot sauce and olive oil. Stir to mix well and add the mushroom pieces. Season with salt and pepper and toss well to mix. Place on a hot grill and cook until soft and slightly charred at the edges. Transfer to a salad bowl and set aside.

2. Add the salad greens and drizzle with vinegar, soy sauce and olive oil. Season lightly with salt and pepper and toss to coat. Serve family style or transfer to four plates and garnish with a sprinkling of sesame seeds and nori.

Warm Salad of Porcini and Barley with Rosemary Vinaigrette

Serves 4

This unusual salad is also great when made with qood quality lentils or white beans. Boletes add an unforgettable dimension to the dish, but the common portobello also gives a great result. The salad can be made in advance, without the mushrooms, and warmed to room temperature before finishing with the freshly sautéed mushrooms.

Vinaigrette

1 tbsp	fresh rosemary, chopped	15 mL
1 tsp	garlic, minced	5 mL
1 tbsp	Dijon mustard	15 mL
2 tbsp	water	30 mL
2 tbsp	sherry vinegar	30 mL
1/4 cup	extra virgin olive oil	60 mL

Salad

1 cup	pearl barley, soaked in water	250 ml
1 cup	carrots, peeled and cubed	250 mL
1 cup	leeks, washed and chopped	250 mL
1 cup	potato, peeled and diced	250 mL
1 tbsp	olive oil	15 mL
1 tbsp	butter	15 mL
1 tbsp	garlic, minced	15 mL
1/2 lb	porcini (bolete) mushrooms, cubed (portobello, white or brown button)	225 g
	salt and pepper to taste	
1/4 cup	shredded ham (optional)	60 mL
	parsley, chopped for garnish	

1. In a salad bowl, combine the rosemary, garlic, mustard, water and vinegar, stir well to mix. Add the oil in a slow and steady stream until incorporated, and set aside until needed.

2. In a stock pot filled with boiling salted water, add barley and cook until just tender, about 25 minutes. Add the carrots, leeks and potato, return to a boil, then reduce heat and simmer until vegetables are tender, about 7–8 minutes. Drain, reserving stock for another use. Add the mixture to the dressing, tossing to coat. Allow to cool.

3. In a non-stick skillet, heat oil over high heat for 45 seconds. Add the garlic and mushrooms. Season well with salt and pepper and sauté until the mushrooms are browned and soft, about 5 minutes. Add to the barley mixture and mix well. To serve, mound salad in the centre of serving plates and garnish with a small pile of shredded ham and a sprinkling of parsley.

Japanese Rice Salad with Morels and Asparagus

Serves 4–6

A variation on a rustic sushi salad that uses short-grain rice tossed with a sweet-and-sour dressing. The result is a chewy rice that readily absorbs the flavour of the mushrooms and complements their texture. I like to mould the rice into oiled ramekins (or small bowls) and unmould them onto a plate garnished with baby lettuce leaves. Nori (sushi seaweed) can be shredded easily with a pair of scissors to make a dramatic garnish on top of the salad.

Sushi Rice

1 cup	short-grain sushi rice	250 mL
2 cups	water	500 mL
1 tbsp	sea salt, divided	15 mL
1/4 cup	rice vinegar	60 mL
2 tbsp	sugar	30 mL

Salad

2 tbsp	pickled ginger, chopped	30 mL
1 tbsp	pickled ginger juice	15 mL
1 tbsp	wasabi paste (or to taste)	15 mL
2 tbsp	light soy sauce	30 mL
2 tbsp	extra virgin olive oil	30 mL
1 tbsp	vegetable oil	15 mL
1 tbsp	garlic, minced	15 mL
1/2 lb	fresh morel mushrooms, halved	225 g
1/2 lb	asparagus, cut on bias	225 g
1/4 cup	chicken or vegetable stock, or water	60 mL
	pickled ginger, shredded for garnish	
	nori, shredded for garnish	

1. In a strainer, place rice and rinse well with water: rub rice to release starch and rinse until water runs clear. To a pot over high heat, add water, rice and half the salt. Bring to a boil and cover. Reduce heat to low and cook for 20 minutes. Remove from heat and allow to sit for an additional 10 minutes. Meanwhile, in a small bowl, combine the vinegar, sugar and remaining salt. Set aside until needed.

2. On a sheet lined with parchment paper, spread the cooked rice and sprinkle with the vinegar mixture. Stir the rice and fluff it up to quickly cool. Allow to cool to room temperature and cover with a clean kitchen towel.

3. In a small bowl, combine the pickled ginger, juice, wasabi and soy sauce. Whisk in the olive oil in a slow stream until smooth. Set aside.

4. In a large non-stick skillet or wok, heat vegetable oil over high for 45 seconds. Add garlic, mushrooms and asparagus and sauté for 3–4 minutes, or until mushrooms are soft and appear dry. Add stock and cook until all moisture is evaporated. Add cooled rice and toss to coat (and reheat slightly). Transfer to a bowl and top with the dressing. Stir well to mix, transfer to plates and garnish with the pickled ginger and nori.

Soy-Marinated Shiitake Mushroom and Rice Noodle Salad

Serves 4–6

This is a simple salad that must be eaten fresh for the best texture. If left to sit for too long the rice noodles will absorb excess moisture and the texture will be soft and starchy. Substitute any cultivated mushroom in place of the shiitake, but increase initial cooking time to 5 minutes.

1 tbsp	vegetable oil	15 mL
1 tbsp	garlic, minced	15 mL
1 tbsp	ginger, minced	15 mL
½ lb	shiitake mushrooms, sliced	225 g
2 tbsp	dark soy sauce	30 mL
1 tsp	hot sauce	5 mL
1 tbsp	brown sugar	15 mL
1 cup	chicken or vegetable stock	250 mL
1 tbsp	cornstarch (mixed with equal water)	15 mL
1	lime, juice and zest	1
2 tbsp	fresh basil (or cilantro), chopped	30 mL
1 lb	fresh thin rice noodles (Lai Fun) (or dried noodles, soaked)	450 g
1 cup	bean sprouts	250 mL
	whole basil leaves for garnish	

1. In a large non-stick skillet or wok, heat oil over high for 45 seconds. Add garlic, ginger and mushrooms and sauté until mushrooms are soft and appear dry, about 2–3 minutes. Add the soy sauce, hot sauce, sugar and stock. Bring to a boil, reduce heat and simmer for 5 minutes. Add the cornstarch, lime zest and juice and basil. Stir until the mixture thickens, then remove from heat and allow to cool.

2. In a pot of boiling salted water, add the noodles and cook for 1–2 minutes, or until soft. Drain and rinse under cold water. Shake well to remove moisture and set aside.

3. In a large bowl, combine the noodles and the mushroom mixture. Toss to mix and serve garnished with bean sprouts and whole basil leaves.

Side Dishes

Chanterelle, Leek and Cheddar Polenta 116

Mushroom and Herb Cornbread 117

Mushroom Yorkshire Pudding 118

Mashed Potatoes with Mushrooms and Garlic 120

Scalloped Potatoes and Mushrooms 122

Smoked Cod and Mushroom Potato Cakes 124

Wild Mushroom, Leek, Goat Cheese and Walnut Risotto 126

Steamed Rice with Wild Mushrooms and Garlic 128

Mushroom, Prosciutto and Barley Pilaf 129

Chanterelle, Leek and Cheddar Polenta

Serves 4–6

Polenta is often served as a bland porridge made from coarsely ground corn. With the proper seasoning this humble peasant dish can be elevated to food for the gods. Using a good quality stock helps to add body and richness to the cornmeal. The starchy flavour also demands that you season the dish heavily with salt and pepper. This is another dish that works with practically every mushroom. Even truffles can be used (sparingly) to infuse the dish with a wonderful flavour.

4 cups	chicken or vegetable stock	1 L
1 cup	white wine	250 mL
1 tbsp	garlic, minced	15 mL
1 tbsp	fresh thyme, minced	15 mL
1 tsp	salt	5 mL
1 cup	leeks, washed and sliced	250 mL
½ lb	chanterelles, diced	225 g
	(button, portobello, morel or bolete)	
1 cup	cornmeal	250 mL
1 cup	aged Cheddar cheese, coarsely grated	250 mL
	salt and pepper to taste	
	extra virgin olive oil for garnish	
	thyme, minced for garnish	
	Parmesan cheese, freshly grated for garnish	

1. In a stock pot, combine stock, white wine, garlic, thyme and salt. Bring to a boil and stir in leeks and chanterelles. Return to a boil, reduce heat and simmer for 5 minutes. While stirring the liquid, add cornmeal in a slow and steady stream. Keep stirring while mixture thickens. Reduce heat and stir occasionally until mixture is smooth, about 7–8 minutes.

2. Add the Cheddar cheese and season well with salt and pepper. Stir well to mix (the mixture should be fairly soft and smooth). Add additional stock or hot water if necessary to thin. Transfer to 4 serving bowls and garnish with a drizzle of extra virgin olive oil, thyme, Parmesan cheese and freshly ground pepper.

Mushroom and Herb Cornbread

Serves 4–6

Another happy marriage of cornmeal and mushrooms, this dish adds a subtle mushroom flavour to crumbly and moist cornbread. For something extra, top the bread with grated Asiago or white Cheddar before baking. This will produce a crisp, yellow crust that will add to the visual appeal and the taste.

Oven: 375°F / 190°C

2 cups	cornmeal	500 mL
1/2 cup	all-purpose flour	125 mL
1 tbsp	dried mushroom powder	15 mL
	(porcini, shiitake, button or mixed)	
1 tsp	cayenne pepper	5 mL
1 tsp	salt	5 mL
1 tbsp	baking powder	15 mL
2 cups	buttermilk (or milk)	500 mL
1	egg, beaten	1
2 tbsp	melted butter (or olive oil)	30 mL
2 cups	mushrooms, minced	500 mL
	(button, cremini or portobello)	
1 cup	corn kernels (fresh or frozen)	250 mL
1/4 cup	assorted fresh herbs, chopped	60 mL
	(parsley, thyme, rosemary, sage, cilantro, etc.)	

1. In a large bowl, combine cornmeal, flour, mushroom powder, cayenne, salt and baking powder. Make a well in the centre and stir in the buttermilk and egg. When smooth, fold in mushrooms, corn and herbs.

2. Into a large cast-iron skillet (buttered and dusted with cornmeal), pour the batter. Shake pan to evenly distribute the batter. Place in a hot oven and bake for 30–40 minutes, or until a toothpick comes out clean from the centre. Transfer to a cooling rack and allow to cool to handling temperature. Cut into thick wedges and serve warm or at room temperature.

Mushroom Yorkshire Pudding

Serves 4–6

The secret of a good Yorkshire pudding is to have all of the ingredients at room temperature before starting. You can cheat, of course, by warming the milk and flour in a microwave oven (for about 1 minute). The warm ingredients cause the pudding to rise faster and reach soufflé-like heights. Once the puddings have risen, do not open the oven door or they will collapse. The puddings must become crispy and golden before they will retain their puffy shape.

Oven: 425°F / 220°C

1 cup	all-purpose flour	250 mL
2 tbsp	dried mushroom powder	30 mL
	(porcini, trumpet, shiitake, button or mixed)	
1 tsp	salt	5 mL
	freshly ground pepper to taste	
4	eggs, beaten	4
1 cup	milk	250 mL
¼ cup	butter, melted	60 mL
¼ cup	vegetable oil	60 mL

1. In a large bowl, combine flour, mushroom powder, salt and pepper. Make a well in the centre and add the eggs and milk. Stir batter to mix well and set aside for at least 10 minutes. The mixture should be of pouring consistency. Thin with additional milk if necessary.

2. Place a 12 cup muffin tin on a baking tray in the hot oven, heat for at least 10 minutes. In a measuring cup, combine the butter and oil. Remove tin from the oven and pour oil mixture into cups with about ¼ in / 1 cm of fat in each. Return to the oven and heat until fat begins to smoke, about 5 minutes.

3. Remove from oven and pour in batter, dividing evenly between cups. Bake for 10 minutes, then reduce heat to 350°F / 180°C and bake for an additional 10 minutes. The Yorkshire puddings should be puffed, brown and crisp. Remove from oven, scoop out of the tin and drain on a paper towel-lined plate. Serve warm with lots of gravy.

Originally Yorkshire pudding was designed as a rustic filler to keep the stomachs full while cutting down the portion of expensive (and rare) meat. The mixture was placed in a pan below a roasted joint of beef. The fat and drippings mingled with the batter and a savoury treat was produced. Now the crispy individual "buns" are mandatory companions to any well-roasted piece of beef.

Mashed Potatoes with Mushrooms and Garlic

Serves 6–8

The smoothness of the mashed potatoes contrasts with the texture of the finely minced mushrooms. Use a starchy white potato to make the best mash. The dish can be elevated to a true culinary work of art with the addition of truffles (or pine mushrooms). If fresh truffles are in season, splurge on a small nugget and thinly slice over top of the finished dish. Use a small mandoline (or Japanese vegetable slicer) to shave whisper-thin slivers of truffle.

2 lb	potatoes, peeled and coarsely chopped	1 kg
3 tbsp	butter, divided	45 mL
1 tbsp	garlic, minced	15 mL
¼ cup	shallots, minced	60 mL
1 cup	mushrooms, minced	250 mL
	(porcini, morel, shiitake or crimini)	
	salt and pepper to taste	
½ cup	milk	125 mL
1 tsp	dried trumpet mushroom powder (optional)	5 mL
	(or chopped black truffle)	

1. To a stock pot filled with cold salted water, add the potatoes and bring to a boil over high heat. Cook until the potatoes are fork-tender, about 8–10 minutes. Strain potatoes in a coarse sieve and set aside to drain for 1 minute.

2. Meanwhile, in a non-stick skillet, heat 1 tbsp / 15 mL butter over high heat for 30 seconds. Add the garlic, shallots and mushrooms. Sauté for 5–6 minutes, or until the shallots and mushrooms are beginning to brown. Remove from heat and set aside to cool. In a small saucepan, warm the milk and the mushroom powder (or truffle).

3. In a large pot, crush the potatoes with a potato ricer (or potato masher) until smooth. Fold in the warm milk and remaining butter and stir over medium heat until butter is melted. Fold in the mushroom mixture. Season with salt and pepper and serve warm.

In my humble opinion, the best way to make mashed potatoes is with a potato ricer. This small device squeezes the potato through a mesh to produce the lightest, finest mash imaginable. Please don't use electric mixers to make the mash. The harsh action causes gluten to form in the potato starch and leaves a gummy texture.

Scalloped Potatoes and Mushrooms

Serves 4

Scalloped potatoes showcase the marriage of mushrooms, potatoes and cream. This dish is great with pine mushrooms, as a small mushroom will infuse a lot of flavour. You can also use a wide variety of dried mushrooms. Add the mushrooms to the cream and allow to infuse with the other flavourings (chop the re-hydrated mushrooms into small pieces — or use ground mushroom powder). The casserole will thicken considerably (and taste better) if the dish is allowed to cool completely. Reheat in the oven until warmed through.

Oven: 350°F / 180°C

4 cups	light cream (or milk)	1 L
2 tbsp	garlic, minced	30 mL
1 tbsp	salt	15 mL
1 tsp	pepper	5 mL
2	whole bay leaves	2
1 tbsp	rosemary, minced	15 mL
1 tbsp	thyme, minced	15 mL
2 lbs	baking potatoes, peeled and sliced	1 kg
1 cup	Gruyère cheese, grated	250 mL
1	small pine mushroom, minced	1
	(or 2 cups / 500 mL sliced cooked mushrooms)	

1. In a large saucepan, combine cream, garlic, salt, pepper, bay leaves, rosemary and thyme. Bring to a boil, remove from heat immediately. Allow to infuse for 15 minutes.

2. Using a vegetable slicer (or mandoline), cut potatoes into very thin slices. Into a large casserole dish, pour a ladle full of cream and top with a layer of potatoes. Sprinkle on some of the mushrooms and a light sprinkling of cheese. Repeat with remaining potatoes, mushrooms, cheese and cream. Pour any remaining cream on top of the potatoes and cover completely (add additional cream or milk if necessary).

3. Place casserole in a hot oven and bake for 1 hour, or until top is browned and potatoes are fork tender. Remove from oven and serve warm. The dish will benefit from sitting for 10 minutes before serving.

Smoked Cod and Mushroom Potato Cakes

Serves 4

These cakes are a great way to use up leftover mashed potatoes. They taste so good I often make the potatoes from scratch just to make the fish cakes. The sherry aïoli contrasts with the smoky fish and complements the crisp cakes.

Sherry Aïoli

1/2 cup	mayonnaise	125 mL
1 tbsp	sweet sherry	15 mL
1 tsp	garlic, minced	5 mL
1 tsp	hot sauce	5 mL
1 tbsp	fresh parsley, minced	15 mL

Fish Cakes

2 tbsp	butter	30 mL
1 tbsp	garlic, minced	15 mL
1/2 lb	white or brown button mushrooms, diced	225 g
	salt and pepper to taste	
4 cups	cold mashed potatoes	1 L
1 cup	smoked black cod (or haddock), chopped	250 mL
1	egg	1
1/2 cup	cornmeal (or bread crumbs)	125 mL
2 tbsp	fresh parsley, finely minced	30 mL
2 tbsp	vegetable oil (or butter)	30 mL
1	lemon, cut in wedges and seeded	1

1. In a small bowl, combine mayonnaise, sherry, garlic, hot sauce and parsley. Stir well to mix and set aside until needed.

2. In a non-stick skillet, heat butter over high heat for 45 seconds. Add garlic and mushrooms and season well with salt and pepper. Sauté until the mushrooms appear dry, about 5 minutes. Allow to cool to handling temperature and reserve.

3. In a large bowl, combine mashed potatoes, cod and mushrooms. Add the egg and gently mix until smooth. Chill until firm, about 10 minutes. On a plate, combine cornmeal and parsley. Season well with salt and pepper. Scoop ½ cup / 125 mL of potato and form into a ball with your hands. Flatten into a round patty and coat both sides with the cornmeal mixture. Place on a baking sheet and chill. Repeat with remaining potato mixture. Can be made up several hours in advance.

4. In a non-stick skillet, heat oil over medium-high heat for 45 seconds. Add 4 potato cakes and fry until golden brown, about 3–4 minutes per side. Transfer to a plate and keep in warm oven until all cakes are cooked. To serve, garnish with a dollop of aïoli and a squeeze of fresh lemon juice.

Try to find a naturally smoked black cod for this dish. You will know the artificially processed cod by the fluorescent red dye used to colour the flesh. Naturally smoked fish will have a golden brown exterior and a sweet smoky aroma.

Wild Mushroom, Leek, Goat Cheese and Walnut Risotto

Serves 4

Native to the foothills of northern Italy, risotto is perfectly matched with fresh plump boletes. Substitute dried mushrooms with excellent results. If your budget can afford it, risotto is another perfect excuse to shave a few curls of truffle. Use a good quality Parmesan cheese for this, grated from a fresh chunk.

1 tbsp	olive oil	15 mL
2 cups	arborio rice (or short-grained rice)	500 mL
½ cup	dry white wine	125 mL
4 cups	chicken or vegetable stock	1 L
1 tbsp	butter (or olive oil)	15 mL
2 cups	sliced leeks	500 mL
1 tbsp	minced garlic	15 mL
2 tbsp	fresh thyme, chopped	30 mL
½ lb	wild mushrooms, sliced	225 g
	(chanterelles, boletes, hedgehogs, morels)	
½ cup	crumbled goat cheese	125 mL
3 tbsp	fresh Italian parsley, minced	45 mL
½ cup	freshly toasted walnuts	125 mL
2 tbsp	Parmesan cheese, grated	30 mL
	extra stock if needed	
	Parmesan cheese for garnish	
	sprigs of fresh Italian parsley for garnish	

1. In a heavy-bottomed saucepan over medium-high heat, add oil and rice. Toss well to coat the grains and cook until rice turns opaque and starts to stick to the bottom. Add wine and stir until the liquid is absorbed. Repeat with stock, 1 cup / 250 mL at a time, stirring constantly and adding more liquid as it is absorbed. The process should take about 20 minutes, or until grains are tender but still firm to the bite.

2. Meanwhile, in a non-stick skillet, heat butter over high heat for 30 seconds. Add the leeks, garlic, thyme and mushrooms. Sauté for 5–6 minutes, or until the leeks and mushrooms are dry and beginning to brown. De-glaze the pan with 2 tbsp / 30 mL of wine, and add vegetables to the risotto.

3. Fold in the goat cheese, Italian parsley, walnuts and Parmesan cheese. Add a little additional stock, if needed, to make a soft, moist risotto. To serve, mound risotto in the centre of serving plates (or pasta bowls) and garnish with additional Parmesan cheese, fresh pepper and a sprig of Italian parsley.

Steamed Rice with Wild Mushrooms and Garlic

Serves 4

Combining two types of rice might seem a little odd, but the combination yields a perfect rice that is fluffy and chewy at the same time. Of course the dish will work with either of the rice types. Feel free to use your favourite rice. The mushrooms tend to discolour the rice (particularly when a black mushroom like the horn of plenty is used). The mushroom powder will tend to float to the top of the rice during cooking. When the dish has finished cooking (and resting), stir with a spatula to distribute the mushrooms throughout the rice.

1 cup	long-grain rice	250 mL
1 cup	short-grain rice	250 mL
4 cups	boiling water	1 L
2 tbsp	ground wild mushroom powder	30 mL
	(porcini, morel, horn of plenty or shiitake)	
8	whole garlic cloves, peeled	8
1 tsp	sea salt	5 mL
2	green onions, thinly sliced	2

1. In a sieve, combine the two types of rice and wash under cold running water. Place sieve in a pot of cold water and let sit for 5 minutes. Meanwhile, in a large bowl, combine the boiling water and the mushroom powder.

2. Drain the rice and shake free of excess moisture. Place in a heavy-bottomed pot with a tight-fitting lid. Add the mushroom stock, garlic and salt, stirring well to mix. Bring to a boil, stir once, cover and reduce heat to low. Simmer for 20 minutes. Remove from heat and allow to sit undisturbed for another 15–20 minutes before opening the lid. Add the green onions and toss gently to mix and fluff the rice.

Mushroom, Prosciutto and Barley Pilaf

Serves 4

Barley is a nutritious grain that is generally underutilized. It will take 30–40 minutes to cook, depending on its age. Old grains will have dehydrated and will need a little more time to absorb the cooking liquid and soften. Buy grains from a good bulk-food store to ensure a good turnover of product. Beef or chicken stock makes a richly flavoured dish. Vegetable or mushroom stock also produces excellent results.

1 1/2 cup	pearl barley	375 mL
4 cups	stock (or boiling water)	1 L
1 tbsp	olive oil	15 mL
1 tbsp	garlic, minced	15 mL
1/2 cup	peeled and sliced shallots	125 mL
1/2 lb	mushrooms, cubed	225 g
	(porcini, portobello, crimini or button)	
	salt and pepper to taste	
4 slices	prosciutto ham, minced	4 slices
2 tbsp	Italian parsley (or basil)	30 mL
2 tbsp	Parmesan cheese	30 mL

1. In a sieve, rinse the barley under cold running water. Place strainer in a pot of cold water and let sit for 5 minutes.

2. In a heavy-bottomed saucepan with a tight-fitting lid, heat olive oil over high heat for 45 seconds. Add the garlic, shallots and mushrooms and season well with salt and pepper. Add the drained barley and stock. Bring to a boil, cover and reduce heat to low. Cook for 40 minutes. Remove from heat and let sit, covered, for an additional 10 minutes.

3. Add the prosciutto, parsley and cheese to the barley and stir well to mix. Serve warm as a side dish or top with sautéed mushrooms as a starter.

Noodles and Pasta

Mushroom, Spinach and Ricotta Lasagna 132

Spaghettini with Mushrooms, Shallots and Garlic 134

Spaghetti with Mushroom-Beef Balls 135

Rice Noodles with Shiitake, Corn and Oyster Sauce 137

Crispy Chow Mein Cake with Mushroom-Wine Sauce 138

Shanghai Noodles with Shredded Mushrooms
and Vegetables 140

Spiced Turkey and Mushrooms over Egg Noodles 142

Mushroom, Spinach and Ricotta Lasagna

Serves 4–6

Lasagna is often one of the first dishes new cooks attempt. It is easy to assemble and an easy way to feed a crowd. Although the dish is good with common button mushrooms, when you add wild mushrooms like chanterelles, this dish becomes something very special. You can easily freeze leftovers in sealable plastic containers.

Oven: 375°F / 190°C

1 lb	lasagna noodles (1 package)	450 g
1 tbsp	vegetable oil	15 mL
	olive oil for drizzling	
1 tbsp	olive oil	15 mL
2 tbsp	garlic, minced	30 mL
3 cups	mushrooms, sliced	750 mL
	(button, portobello, chanterelles, oysters, etc.)	
	salt and pepper to taste	
4 cups	mushroom-tomato sauce (page 62)	1 L
2 cups	ricotta cheese	500 mL
1 lb	spinach leaves, cleaned and stemmed	450 g
2 cups	mozzarella cheese, coarsely grated	500 mL

1. To a large pot filled with boiling salted water, add pasta and vegetable oil. Stir occasionally until noodles soften and separate. Cook until *al dente*, about 7–8 minutes. Remove from heat, strain through a colander and shake well to remove excess water. Drizzle pasta with a little olive oil and toss gently to separate the sheets.

2. In a large non-reactive saucepan over medium-high heat, add olive oil, garlic and mushrooms. Stir well, season with salt and pepper and cook until mushrooms appear dry, about 5 minutes. Add tomato sauce, stir well and bring to a boil. Remove from heat and stir in spinach. Allow to wilt, about 2 minutes.

3. Oil a large, deep casserole dish and ladle a thin layer of sauce on the bottom. Top with a layer of noodles and then a thick layer of tomato sauce. Sprinkle 1/3 of the ricotta on top and repeat with layers of pasta, sauce and cheese. Spoon any leftover sauce on top of the lasagna and sprinkle shredded mozzarella cheese on top. Bake in a hot oven for 20–25 minutes, or until cheese is bubbling and starting to brown. Remove from oven. Allow to rest for 5–10 minutes before cutting into portions.

Spaghettini with Mushrooms, Shallots and Garlic

Serves 4

We commonly think of spaghetti slathered with tomato sauce. In Italy, you are just as likely to have pasta dressed in olive oil, garlic and cheese. This dish delivers with a truly satisfying blend of simple seasonings. It can be made in 15 minutes and is a complete meal when served with a simple salad.

1 lb	dry spaghettini (or angel hair pasta)	450 g
1 tbsp	vegetable oil	15 mL
	olive oil for drizzling	
2 tbsp	olive oil	30 mL
2	medium shallots, diced	2
1 tbsp	garlic, minced	15 mL
2 cups	mushrooms, diced	500 mL
	(button, porcini, chanterelle, oyster, etc.)	
	salt and pepper to taste	
1 tbsp	fresh rosemary (or sage), minced	15 mL
2 tbsp	Parmesan cheese, grated	30 mL
	additional Parmesan cheese for garnish	

1. To a large pot filled with boiling salted water, add spaghettini and vegetable oil. Stir occasionally until noodles soften and separate. Cook until *al dente*, about 5–6 minutes. Remove from heat, strain through a colander and shake well to remove excess water. Drizzle noodles with a little olive oil and toss gently to separate strands.

2. Meanwhile, in a large non-stick skillet over medium-high heat, mix olive oil, shallots and garlic. Stir until shallots start browning, then add mushrooms and rosemary. Season well with salt and pepper and sauté until mushrooms are soft and appear dry, about 5 minutes.

3. Add the cooked pasta to the skillet, tossing well with 2 wooden spoons. Sprinkle on the Parmesan cheese and toss to coat. Season well with lots of freshly ground black pepper. Transfer to 4 pasta bowls and top each bowl with additional Parmesan cheese.

Spaghetti with Mushroom-Beef Balls

Serves 4

This is pasta in a more traditional style and the dish can be prepared with homemade mushroom-tomato sauce or your favourite store-bought product. The mushrooms add great texture and flavour to the meatballs. For a stronger mushroom flavour, add a spoonful of dried mushroom powder to the raw meat.

Oven: 375°F / 190°C

Meatballs

1/2 lb	ground beef (or turkey)	225 g
2 cups	mushrooms, diced	500 mL
	(button, cremini, porcini, chanterelle, etc.)	
1 cup	bread, cubed	250 mL
1	small onion, minced	1
1 tbsp	garlic, minced	15 mL
1 tsp	hot sauce	5 mL
3 tbsp	fresh herbs, chopped	45 mL
	(parsley, basil, chives and/or lovage)	
1	egg, slightly beaten	1
	salt and pepper to taste	

Spaghetti

4 cups	mushroom-tomato sauce (page 62)	1 L
1 lb	dry spaghetti	450 g
1 tbsp	vegetable oil	15 mL
	Parmesan cheese for garnish	

cont'd on page 136

1. In a medium bowl, combine beef, mushrooms, bread, onion, garlic, hot sauce and herbs. Season well with salt and pepper and add egg. With clean hands, mix until smooth. Shape into small balls and place on a baking sheet. Repeat with remaining mixture. Season with salt and pepper and bake until golden brown, about 15 minutes.

2. Meanwhile, in a medium non-reactive saucepan, bring mushroom-tomato sauce to a boil. Reduce heat to low and simmer until needed. To a large pot filled with boiling, salted water, add spaghetti and vegetable oil. Stir occasionally until noodles soften and separate. Cook until *al dente*, about 6–7 minutes. Remove from heat, strain through a colander and shake well to remove excess water. Drizzle noodles with a little olive oil and toss gently to separate strands.

3. Return noodles to the pot, top with sauce and toss well to coat. Transfer pasta to a serving platter or individual bowls, and top with the warm meatballs. Serve garnished with a sprinkling of Parmesan cheese.

Roll the meatballs into bite-size portions (occasionally cleaning and lightly oiling your hands helps to form smooth meatballs). You can freeze the raw meatballs in packages of 12 and cook when defrosted. Alternatively, you can bake the meatballs, combine with sauce and freeze together.

Rice Noodles with Shiitake, Corn and Oyster Sauce

Serves 4

Rice noodles make perfect fast food. This sauce is ready in under 15 minutes and the noodles cook in a matter of seconds. Shiitake mushrooms seem to work the best in this dish. The strong flavour contrasts well with the bland rice noodles. Be sure not to overcook the rice noodles. If left to sit, the noodles continue to absorb moisture and can become quite starchy.

1 tbsp	vegetable oil	15 mL
1 tbsp	garlic, minced	15 mL
1 tbsp	ginger, minced	15 mL
1	onion, chopped	1
2 cups	stock	500 mL
2 tbsp	oyster sauce	30 mL
1 tsp	hot sauce	5 mL
16	shiitake mushroom caps, thickly sliced	16
1 cup	frozen or fresh corn kernels	250 mL
1 tbsp	cornstarch	15 mL
	(dissolved in an equal amount of water)	
1 lb	fresh flat rice noodles	450 g
	(or any rice noodle or strand pasta)	
2 tbsp	fresh cilantro, chopped	30 mL

1. In a wok or large non-stick skillet over medium-high heat, heat oil for 45 seconds. Add garlic, ginger and onions and sauté until the onions brown, about 3–4 minutes. Add stock, oyster sauce, hot sauce, mushrooms and corn. Bring to a boil, reduce heat and simmer until mushrooms are tender, about 5 minutes.

2. Add cornstarch mixture to the skillet and stir until thickened, about 1 minute. In a colander, place rice noodles and run under hot water until strands separate and begin to soften. Add noodles to sauce and toss well to mix and heat noodles through. Transfer to a serving plate, garnish with cilantro and serve immediately.

Crispy Chow Mein Cake Topped with Mushroom-Wine Sauce

Serves 4

Fresh chow mein noodles are becoming widely available in large grocery stores. Don't use the deep-fried version; these are mainly used for garnish and salad croutons. Be sure to fluff the noodles before placing in the oven; this will crisp the strands and make a beautiful presentation. You can use fresh angel hair pasta as a substitute, boiling the noodles until *al dente*.

Oven: 375°F / 180°C

Crispy Noodles

1 lb	fresh chow mein noodles	450 g
	vegetable oil for drizzling	
	salt and pepper to taste	

Mushroom Sauce

2 tbsp	vegetable oil, divided	30 mL
2 tbsp	garlic, minced	30 mL
½ lb	mushrooms, sliced	225 g
	(button, shiitake, oyster, chanterelle, cauliflower)	
1 cup	white wine	250 mL
2 cups	vegetable stock	500 mL
1 tbsp	cornstarch	15 mL
	(dissolved in an equal amount of water)	
1 tbsp	fresh thyme, chopped	15 mL
2 cups	sui choy (or cabbage), shredded	500 mL
1 cup	bean sprouts	250 mL

1. To a large heat-proof bowl, add chow mein noodles and cover with boiling water. Allow to sit for 3–4 minutes. Drain well, drizzle with a little vegetable oil and toss to coat.

2. In a non-stick skillet over high heat, add 1 tbsp / 15 mL oil and heat for 45 seconds. Add drained noodles, season with salt and pepper and toss gently. Fry until golden brown and crispy on the bottom. Flip noodles, separate strands and transfer to a baking sheet. Bake in a hot oven until crisp and brown, about 10 minutes.

3. Meanwhile, in a wok or large non-stick skillet over medium-high heat, heat remaining oil for 45 seconds. Add garlic and mushrooms and sauté until mushrooms appear dry, about 5 minutes. Add white wine and cook until volume has reduced by half, about 4–5 minutes. Add stock and bring to a boil.

4. Add cornstarch and stir until sauce thickens, about 1 minute. Add thyme and sui choy. Stir until vegetables are soft, about 1–2 minutes. Add bean sprouts, stir to mix and season with salt and pepper. To serve, place the crispy noodles on a large serving platter and top with the hot mushroom sauce.

Shanghai Noodles with Shredded Mushrooms and Vegetables

Serves 4

Shanghai noodles are thick strands of pasta that have a pleasing chewy texture. You can substitute fresh spaghetti or dried ziti pasta. This is a great wintertime dish when carrots and cabbage are the closest thing to fresh, local vegetables. Try to find sweet soy sauce in your local Asian market. It is a rich, sweet sauce made with the addition of sugar cane, and is generally imported from Indonesia. A good teriyaki sauce will also work well.

1 tbsp	vegetable oil	15 mL
1 tbsp	ginger, minced	15 mL
1	small jalapeño, seeded and minced	1
1	small onion, sliced	1
1	large carrot, julienned	1
2 cups	mushrooms, julienned	500 mL
	(button, crimini, portobello, oyster)	
2 cups	cabbage, shredded	500 mL
1 lb	Shanghai noodles	450 g
	(or round rice noodles or strand pasta)	
	vegetable oil for drizzling	
2 tbsp	sweet (or dark) soy sauce	30 mL
1 cup	bean sprouts	250 mL
2 tbsp	fresh cilantro, chopped	30 mL
	additional cilantro for garnish	

1. In a wok or large non-stick skillet over medium-high heat, add oil and heat for 45 seconds. Add ginger, jalapeño and onion, carrots, mushrooms and cabbage. Stir-fry until vegetables just begin to soften, about 4–5 minutes. Reduce heat to low and keep warm until needed.

2. Meanwhile, to a pot filled with boiling salted water, add noodles and cook until soft and warmed through, about 4–5 minutes. Drain in a colander and shake to remove excess water. Drizzle noodles with oil and toss well to coat.

3. Add drained noodles to wok and toss with vegetables. Season with soy sauce; add bean sprouts and cilantro. Toss well to mix and transfer to a serving platter. Garnish with sprigs of cilantro and serve immediately.

Spiced Turkey and Mushrooms over Egg Noodles

Serves 4

Turkey is a vastly underutilized meat. The problem of buying a whole bird has been addressed with the sale of turkey parts. Stewing really helps to tenderize tougher cuts like thighs. The rich flavour of the broth needs a strongly flavoured mushroom like the portobello or chanterelle. Cut the mushrooms into thick slices, similar in size to the turkey pieces.

1 lb	turkey meat, cut in chunks	450 g
	(boneless, skinless thigh and/or breast)	
1 tsp	ground cumin	5 mL
1 tsp	ground coriander	5 mL
1 tsp	ground cinnamon	5 mL
1 tsp	chili flakes	5 mL
	salt and pepper to taste	
2 tbsp	flour (or cornstarch)	30 mL
2 tbsp	vegetable oil, divided	30 mL
½ lb	mushrooms, thickly sliced	225 g
	(portobello, chanterelle, porcini, brown button)	
2 cups	chicken (or mushroom) stock	500 mL
8	baby bok choy, quartered	8
1 tbsp	cornstarch	15 mL
	(dissolved in an equal amount of water)	
½ lb	egg noodles	225 g
	vegetable oil for drizzling	
1 tbsp	chopped fresh parsley (or cilantro)	15 mL

1. In a medium bowl, combine turkey, cumin, coriander, cinnamon and chili flakes. Season well with salt and pepper; sprinkle on flour and toss well to coat.

2. In a non-stick skillet over high heat, heat 1 tbsp / 15 mL oil for 45 seconds. Add turkey and stir-fry over high heat for 2–3 minutes. Add mushrooms and sauté until they start to brown, about 5 minutes. Add stock, bring to a boil, reduce heat and simmer for 5 minutes. Add bok choy and bring back to a boil. Add cornstarch and stir until mixture thickens. Reduce heat to low and keep warm.

3. To a large pot filled with boiling salted water, add egg noodles and cook until soft, about 3–4 minutes. Drain in a colander and shake to remove excess water. Drizzle noodles with oil and toss well to coat.

4. In a deep casserole dish or serving bowl, place warm noodles and top with the turkey sauce. Garnish with chopped parsley.

Vegetarian Main Courses

Portobello and Green Onion Pancakes with Plum Sauce 146

Mushroom Polenta with Spicy Mushroom-Corn Sauce 148

Chanterelle and Aged Cheddar Frittata 150

Grilled Peppers and Mushrooms with Peanut Curry Sauce 152

Chanterelle Cabbage Rolls with Star Anise Tomato Sauce 154

Morel, New Potato, Asparagus and Asiago Gratin 156

Sautéed Oyster Mushrooms and Pea Tops 158

Crispy Potato-Onion Pancakes with Mushroom Gravy 159

Stir-fried Vegetables and Mushrooms in Black Bean Sauce 161

Portobello and Green Onion Pancakes with Plum Sauce

Serves 4–6

Mushroom pancakes are unusual and very tasty. Use fresh, brown-gilled portobello mushrooms. Make small bite-size pancakes for appetizers or large pancakes for a hearty meal. You can buy plum sauce in many grocery stores, or you can make your own by stewing fresh plums with a little ginger and just enough water to make a sauce.

Oven: 200°F / 95°C

Plum Sauce

1/2 cup	plum sauce	125 mL
1	lemon, juice of	1
1 tbsp	soy sauce	15 mL
1 tsp	hot sauce	5 mL

Portobello Pancakes

1 cup	all-purpose flour	250 mL
1 tsp	ground mushroom powder (page 57)	5 mL
2 tsp	baking powder	10 mL
1 tsp	salt	5 mL
1	egg	1
2 tbsp	ice water	30 mL
2 cups	portobello mushrooms, julienned (button, chanterelle, oyster or porcini)	500 mL
1 cup	cabbage, thinly shredded	250 mL
4	green onions, sliced olive oil for pan-frying	4

1. In a small bowl, combine plum sauce, lemon juice, soy sauce and hot sauce. Stir well to mix and set aside until needed.

2. In a medium bowl, sift together flour, mushroom powder, baking powder and salt. Make a well in the centre, add egg and ice water. Whisk the mixture slowly, to gradually incorporate flour until smooth. Fold in the mushrooms, cabbage and green onions.

3. In a non-stick skillet, heat 1 tbsp / 15 mL oil over high for 45 seconds. Add a spoonful of batter to the pan. Spread out to make a small round pancake. Make 3 more pancakes and cook for 2–3 minutes per side, or until crisp and golden. Transfer to a plate lined with paper towel, and place in a warm oven. To serve, place pancakes on a serving platter with sauce on the side.

It's easy to julienne a large-capped mushroom such as the portobello. Cut off the stem (discard if woody or decayed); cut the cap sideways into 2–3 thin slices; cut the slices into thin strips. One large portobello mushroom will give you about 2 cups of julienned mushrooms.

Mushroom Polenta
with Spicy Mushroom-Corn Sauce

Serves 4

Polenta is often served as a bland lump of cooked cornmeal. I like to add texture and flavour by adding vegetables and ground mushroom powder. If allowed to cool, the polenta will form a solid mass that is easy to cut into a variety of shapes. Cookie or biscuit cutters work well to turn the humble polenta into a beautiful circle, heart or your own favourite shape. I like to use my lovely maple leaf-shaped cutter.

Polenta

6 cups	water (or stock)	1.5 L
1 tbsp	salt	15 mL
2 cups	cornmeal	500 mL
2 tbsp	ground mushroom powder (page 57)	30 mL
2 cups	sui choy (or cabbage), chopped	500 mL
2 tbsp	butter (or olive oil)	30 mL
1/4 cup	Parmesan cheese, grated	60 mL
	salt and pepper to taste	

Mushroom Corn Sauce

2 tbsp	olive oil	30 mL
1 cup	onion, diced	250 mL
1 tbsp	garlic, minced	15 mL
1 tbsp	fresh rosemary (or sage), minced	15 mL
2 cups	button mushrooms, diced	500 mL
1 cup	fresh or frozen corn kernels	250 mL
2 cups	mushroom (or other) stock	500 mL
1 tbsp	cornstarch	15 mL
	(dissolved in an equal amount of water)	
1 tsp	chili paste	5 mL
1 tsp	chili oil	5 mL
	green onions for garnish, chopped	

1. To a heavy-bottomed pot over medium-high heat, add water and salt. Bring to a rolling boil and slowly pour in the cornmeal and mushroom powder. Stir until mixture begins to thicken; lower heat and continue to cook for 10 minutes, stirring occasionally. Fold in sui choy, butter and Parmesan. Stir well to mix and cook for another 4–5 minutes, or until the sui choy has wilted. Pour into a buttered casserole dish and allow to cool slightly.

2. Meanwhile, in a non-stick skillet over medium-high heat, add oil and heat for 45 seconds. Add onion, garlic, rosemary and mushrooms, and season well with salt and pepper. Cook until the mushrooms are soft, about 5 minutes. Add the corn and stock and bring to a boil. Pour in the cornstarch mixture and stir until thickened. Season with chili paste and chili oil.

3. To serve, cut the polenta into slices with a sharp knife. Cut the slices on the bias to make 2 triangles. Warm polenta in an oven or microwave, and place 3 triangles on each plate and top with the mushroom-corn sauce, and garnish with green onions.

Chanterelle and Aged Cheddar Frittata

Serves 4

Eggs and mushrooms are magic when cooked together. I have many fond memories of mushroom foraging that ended with a simple omelet. A frittata is the Italian version of an omelet. The egg is topped with cheese and baked, as opposed to the French style of folding the cooked egg. Gently cook the eggs over moderate heat to create the finest texture. The water beaten with the eggs helps to guarantee a fluffy and soft frittata. To make a full and satisfying meal, serve the omelet with pan-fried potatoes and toast.

Oven: 350°F / 180°C

6	eggs, slightly beaten	6
2 tbsp	cold water	30 mL
2 tbsp	fresh parsley, minced	30 mL
1 tbsp	fresh sage, minced	15 mL
	salt and pepper to taste	
1 tbsp	butter (or olive oil)	15 mL
2	medium shallots, diced	2
1 tsp	garlic, minced	5 mL
½ lb	chanterelle mushrooms, sliced	225 g
	(porcini, oyster, shiitake, portobello or button)	
1 cup	aged Cheddar cheese (or Asiago), grated	250 mL

1. In a medium bowl, whisk together eggs, cold water, parsley and sage. Season well with salt and pepper and set aside.

2. In an oven-proof skillet, heat butter over high heat for 45 seconds. Add shallots, garlic and chanterelles. Season well with salt and pepper and sauté until the mushrooms begin to brown, about 5 minutes. Pour eggs over mushrooms and stir well with a spatula. When the eggs just begin to set, smooth with a spatula and top with cheese.

3. Transfer to a hot oven and bake for 5 minutes. To serve, cut the omelet into large wedges and remove with a spatula.

Grilled Peppers and Mushrooms with Peanut Curry Sauce

Serves 4

Oyster mushrooms are transformed when cooked on a hot grill. The sweetness of the peppers contrasts well with the slightly bitter edge of the mushrooms. Feel free to use additional hot sauce. A handful of chopped dry-roasted peanuts adds a crunchy garnish.

Grill: Hot

1 tbsp	vegetable oil	15 mL
1 tbsp	ginger, minced	15 mL
1 tbsp	garlic, minced	15 mL
1	medium onion, diced	1
2 tsp	curry paste	10 mL
½ cup	coconut milk	125 mL
½ cup	peanut butter	125 mL
1 cup	hot stock (or water)	250 mL
1	lime, juice of	1
2 tbsp	fresh cilantro (or basil), minced	30 mL
2	ripe peppers, peeled and quartered (red, yellow, orange, purple, etc.)	2
½ lb	oyster mushrooms	225 g
1 tbsp	olive oil	15 mL
	salt and pepper to taste	
	additional chopped fresh herbs for garnish (or dry-roasted peanuts, chopped)	

1. In a non-stick skillet over medium-high heat, add oil and heat for 45 seconds. Add ginger, garlic and onions and sauté until the onions begin to soften and brown, about 2–3 minutes. Add curry paste and sauté until fragrant. Add coconut milk and peanut butter and stir to dissolve. Thin with hot stock until the mixture reaches a sauce consistency. Season with lime juice, cilantro, salt and pepper. Set aside and keep warm until needed.

2. In a small bowl, place the peppers and drizzle with olive oil and season with salt and pepper. Repeat with mushrooms in a separate bowl. Place vegetables on hot grill, beginning with peppers, and cook until they are soft and slightly charred on both sides. Peppers will take 5–6 minutes, mushrooms 2–3 minutes. Transfer vegetables back to the bowl when cooked.

3. To serve, mound vegetables on a serving platter and top with curry sauce. Garnish with chopped herbs or dry-roasted peanuts and serve warm with steamed rice or cooked noodles.

Chanterelle Cabbage Rolls with
Star Anise Tomato Sauce

Serves 4

Cabbage rolls are a classic comfort food. Barley adds a nutty, chewy texture to the dish, but rice works equally well. The licorice flavour of the star anise works particularly well with the tomato sauce. The intense flavour of fresh star anise can overpower the other seasonings, so keep tasting the sauce and remove the star anise when spiced enough.

Oven: 375°F / 190°C

Tomato Sauce

2 cups	tomato juice	500 mL
1	whole star anise (or 1⁄2 tsp / 2 mL ground)	1
1 tbsp	ginger, minced	15 mL
1 tbsp	dark soy sauce	15 mL
2 tbsp	brown sugar	30 mL
2 tbsp	fresh Thai (or regular) basil, minced	30 mL
2 tbsp	rice vinegar	30 mL
1 tsp	hot sauce	5 mL
	salt and pepper to taste	

Cabbage Rolls

1	head green cabbage, cored	1
1 cup	leeks, washed and chopped	250 mL
1⁄2 lb	chanterelles, chopped	225 g
	(button, portobello, porcini or oyster)	
2 tbsp	garlic, minced	30 mL
2 cups	cooked rice (or pearl barley)	500 mL
2 tbsp	fresh basil, minced	30 mL

1. In a saucepan, combine tomato juice, star anise, ginger, soy sauce, sugar, basil, rice vinegar and hot sauce. Bring to a boil, reduce heat to low and simmer for 15 minutes. Strain, set aside and keep warm until needed.

2. In a large pot filled with boiling salted water, carefully place the head of cabbage. As the leaves begin to soften and appear translucent, pry from the head and remove with a pair of tongs. Place leaves in a bowl of ice water to cool. Transfer to a sheet lined with paper towels and repeat until you have 12 leaves.

3. In a non-stick pan over medium-high heat, add oil and heat for 45 seconds. Add leeks, chanterelles and garlic. Season well with salt and pepper and sauté until the mushrooms appear dry, about 5 minutes. Transfer to a medium bowl and combine with the rice and basil. Stir well to mix.

4. On a flat work surface, place a cabbage leaf and fill with a 1/2 cup / 125 mL rice mixture. Fold over stem side of the leaf, trim rib if it is too thick to roll. Fold in the 2 sides and roll into a tight cylinder. Place in a casserole dish and repeat with remaining cabbage and filling. Top with tomato sauce and bake in a hot oven for 30 minutes, or until cabbage is soft and the sauce is bubbling. Remove from oven and allow to cool slightly before serving.

Morel, New Potato, Asparagus and Asiago Gratin

Serves 4

Morels are a welcome sign that spring has arrived and the delights of summer are just around the corner. The morels absorb flavours and sauces through their sponge-like surfaces. A true springtime dish, this recipe uses fresh local asparagus and new potatoes.

Oven: 400°F / 200°C

2 tbsp	butter (or olive oil)	30 mL
2 cups	morel mushrooms, sliced	500 mL
1 cup	leeks, sliced	250 mL
2 tbsp	garlic, minced	30 mL
½ lb	asparagus, trimmed and sliced	225 g
	salt and pepper to taste	
2 tbsp	flour	30 mL
1 cup	white wine	250 mL
2 cups	milk (or cream)	500 mL
1 lb	new nugget potatoes	450 g
¼ cup	fresh chives, chopped	60 mL
1 cup	Asiago (or Swiss) cheese, shredded	250 mL

1. In a non-stick pan over medium-high heat, add butter and heat for 45 seconds. Add morels, leeks, garlic and asparagus. Season well with salt and pepper and sauté until the mushrooms appear dry, about 5 minutes. Sprinkle vegetables with flour and stir well to mix. Add a little additional butter if the mixture appears too dry. Add wine and cook until the mixture thickens. Add milk and simmer for 5 minutes, stirring occasionally.

2. Meanwhile, to a large pot filled with boiling salted water, add potatoes and cook until just tender. Drain and allow to cool to handling temperature. Cut potatoes in half (larger ones into quarters) and place in a buttered casserole dish. Sprinkle chives on top and set aside until needed.

3. Pour thickened sauce over potatoes and toss to coat. Sprinkle the cheese on top and place in hot oven. Bake for 10–15 minutes, or until the cheese is bubbling and beginning to brown. Allow to rest for 5 minutes before serving.

Sautéed Oyster Mushrooms and Pea Tops

Serves 4

Pea tops are a fairly recent addition to our supermarket shelves. For years we have neglected the sweet leaves and tendrils of the plant in favour of the more obvious pods. It turns out we were missing quite a treat. The soft leaves are reminiscent of spinach, with a mild pea flavour.

1 tbsp	vegetable oil	15 mL
1 cup	onions, diced	250 mL
1 tbsp	ginger, minced	15 mL
1 tsp	curry paste	5 mL
2 cups	vegetable stock	500 mL
1 tbsp	cornstarch	15 mL
	(dissolved in an equal amount of water)	
1 lb	oyster mushrooms, trimmed	450 g
	(button, chanterelle, morels, portobello)	
4 cups	pea tops (or chopped spinach)	1 L
	salt and pepper to taste	
1 tsp	sesame oil	5 mL
1 tsp	chili oil (or hot sauce)	5 mL

1. In a wok or large non-stick pan over medium-high heat, add oil and heat for 45 seconds. Add onions and ginger and sauté until onions start to brown, about 3–4 minutes. Add curry paste and stir until fragrant. Pour in stock and bring to a boil. Reduce heat, add cornstarch and stir constantly until the mixture thickens.

2. Add oyster mushrooms and cook until soft, about 2–3 minutes. Add pea tops and season with salt, pepper, sesame oil and chili oil. Toss to coat and, when wilted, transfer to a platter and serve immediately.

Crispy Potato-Onion Pancakes with Mushroom Gravy

Serves 4–6

The trick to making great potato pancakes is to use large baking potatoes and grate them just before cooking. The potato starch helps to bind the pancakes together and results in crisp, golden pancakes. You can make small, fist-size pancakes for maximum crunch or you can make a large, pan-size cake and cut into wedges to serve. Flipping the large pancake can be tricky. Use a plate to cover the frying pan and flip the cake onto the plate. Slide the pancake back into the pan and continue cooking. The pancakes can be made in advance and reheated in a hot oven until crisp, about 10 minutes.

Oven: 200°F / 95°C

Gravy

2 tbsp	butter (or olive oil)	30 mL
1 cup	onion, diced	250 mL
1 cup	button mushrooms, diced	250 mL
1 tsp	ground mushroom powder (page 57)	5 mL
1 tbsp+	flour (heaping spoonful)	15 mL+
1 tbsp	sherry (or brandy) optional	15 mL
2 cups	mushroom (or vegetable) stock	500 mL
1 tbsp	dark soy sauce	15 mL
	salt and pepper to taste	

Pancakes

4	large potatoes, peeled and grated	4
1	small onion, shredded	1
1 tbsp	olive oil	15 mL
1 tbsp	fresh rosemary, chopped	15 mL
1 tbsp	fresh sage, chopped	15 mL
1 tbsp	potato starch (or flour)	15 mL
	salt and pepper to taste	
	additional vegetable oil for frying	

cont'd on page 160

1. In a non-stick skillet over medium-high heat, add oil and heat for 45 seconds. Add onions and sauté until soft, about 3–4 minutes. Add mushrooms and sauté until mushrooms appear dry, about 5 minutes. Add mushroom powder and flour to pan and stir well to mix. Add sherry and stock to the pan and stir until the mixture thickens, about 3–4 minutes. Reduce heat to low and simmer for 5 minutes. Season with the soy sauce, and salt and pepper, and keep warm until needed.

2. In a medium bowl, combine potatoes, onion, olive oil, rosemary, sage and potato starch. Season with salt and pepper. In a non-stick pan over medium-high, heat 1 tbsp / 15 mL of vegetable oil and spoon 4 small pancakes into the pan. Reduce heat to medium and fry until golden brown, about 3–4 minutes per side. Transfer to a baking sheet and place in a warm oven. Repeat with remaining potato mixture.

3. To serve, place a stack of potato cakes on a plate and cover with a little mushroom gravy, or serve family style on a warm platter with the sauce on the side.

Stir-fried Vegetables and Mushrooms
in Black Bean Sauce

Serves 4

Stir-fries are a quick and efficient way to bring dinner to the table. I like to use a non-stick wok for problem-free cooking and cleaning. The black bean sauce is quite pungent and can overpower the flavour of wild mushrooms, so use any cultivated mushroom for best results.

2 tbsp	vegetable oil	30 mL
1 tbsp	garlic, minced	15 mL
1 tbsp	ginger, minced	15 mL
1 cup	carrots, peeled and thinly sliced	250 mL
2 cups	mushrooms, sliced	500 mL
	(button, portobello, oyster, shiitake)	
2 cups	broccoli florets	500 mL
2 cups	cauliflower florets	500 mL
1 cup	snow peas	250 mL
2 tbsp	black bean sauce	30 mL
2 cups	stock	500 mL
1 tbsp	cornstarch	15 mL
	(dissolved in an equal amount of water)	
1 tsp	sesame oil	5 mL
1 tbsp	toasted sesame seeds	15 mL

1. In a wok or large non-stick skillet over medium-high heat, add oil and heat for 45 seconds. Add garlic, ginger and carrots and sauté until soft, about 3–4 minutes. Add the mushrooms and sauté until the mushrooms appear dry, about 5 minutes.

2. Add broccoli, cauliflower and peas. Stir-fry for 2–3 minutes and add the black bean sauce. Toss well to coat and cook for 1–2 minutes. Add stock to the pan and stir well to dissolve the bean sauce. Add cornstarch and stir until mixture thickens, about 1 minute. Season with salt, pepper and sesame oil. Transfer to a serving platter and garnish with sesame seeds.

Seafood Dishes

Pan-fried Shiitake Mushrooms and Scallops in Rice Paper 164

Mushroom and Seafood Risotto 166

Trout Rolls Stuffed with Morel-Potato Mousse 168

Baked Portobello Caps Stuffed with Shrimp Cocktail 170

Salmon, Pepper and Mushroom Ragout 171

Mussels and Clams in Chardonnay Pine Mushroom Sauce 173

Smoked Sablefish and Chanterelles Braised in
Tomato-Lemon Broth 174

Grilled Portobello and Halibut with Miso-Honey Glaze 175

Pan-fried Shiitake Mushrooms and Scallops in Rice Paper

Serves 4

These tasty bundles make an elegant presentation for a special dinner party. The scallops, cooked lightly (steamed inside the bundle), will be juicy and plump. If you desire the scallops cooked completely through, transfer to a hot oven and roast for another 5 minutes. The scallops should be fresh and free of any fishy odour.

Dressing

1 tbsp	mustard	15 mL
1 tbsp	light soy sauce	15 mL
1 tsp	hot sauce	5 mL
1 tbsp	rice vinegar	15 mL
3 tbsp	vegetable oil	45 mL

Scallops

12	large sea scallops	12
24	large shiitake mushroom caps	24
1 tbsp	garlic, minced	15 mL
1 tbsp	fresh cilantro (or basil), minced	15 mL
1 tsp	sesame oil	5 mL
1 tbsp	light soy sauce	15 mL
	salt and pepper to taste	
12	small circles of rice paper	12
1 tbsp	vegetable (or olive) oil	15 mL
	fresh cilantro sprigs for garnish	

1. In a small bowl, combine mustard, soy sauce, hot sauce and rice vinegar. Add the oil in a slow and steady stream until the mixture appears smooth. Set aside until needed.

2. In a medium bowl, combine scallops, mushrooms, garlic, cilantro, sesame oil and soy sauce. Season well with salt and pepper and toss to mix.

3. In a small skillet half-filled with hot water, place a sheet of rice paper and allow to soak until soft and pliable, about 1 minute. Remove the sheet from the water as soon as it softens (note: very hot water will work quickly; the process will slow as the water cools). Carefully lift sheet using your fingers, and place on a flat work surface.

4. Place a mushroom cap in the middle of a small rice paper circle, gill-side up. Top with a scallop, then a second mushroom, gill-side down (to form a sandwich). Fold over 1 side of the rice paper and repeat with opposite side. Fold over remaining sides to form a smooth bundle. Place seam-side down on a plate and repeat with remaining ingredients. May be refrigerated for 1–2 hours, tightly covered with plastic wrap.

5. In a non-stick pan over medium-high heat, add oil and heat for 30 seconds. Add 4 bundles at a time, season with salt and pepper and fry until golden, about 2–3 minutes per side. Transfer to a platter and reserve in a warm oven until all bundles are cooked. Drizzle the warm bundles with the dressing and garnish with fresh cilantro sprigs.

Mushroom and Seafood Risotto

Serves 4

Add the seafood just before serving and just warm through for best results. A wide variety of fresh seafood can be used. For a golden-coloured risotto and flavour that complements the seafood, add a pinch of dried saffron at the start.

2 tbsp	olive oil	30 mL
2 cups	arborio rice (or short-grain rice)	500 mL
1 tbsp	garlic, minced	15 mL
4	shallots, minced	4
2 cups	mushrooms, sliced	500 mL
	(button, shiitake, oyster, chanterelle)	
1 cup	white wine	250 mL
4 cups	stock (or water)	1 L
4 cups	mixed seafood	1 L
	(prawns, scallops, salmon, squid, fish cubes)	
1	small pine mushroom, sliced (optional)	1
2 tbsp	fresh Italian parsley, minced	30 mL
2 cups	spinach leaves, washed and stemmed	500 mL
2 tbsp	Parmesan cheese	30 mL
1	green onion, thinly sliced	1
	salt and pepper to taste	
	additional Parmesan cheese for garnish	

1. In a heavy-bottomed pot over medium-high heat, add oil and rice. Toss well to coat grains and cook until rice turns opaque and starts to stick to the bottom, about 5 minutes. Add the garlic, shallots and mushrooms and cook for 2–3 minutes. Add wine and stir until the liquid is almost completely evaporated. Add stock 1 cup / 250 mL at a time, stirring occasionally and adding more liquid as it is absorbed. The process should take about 20 minutes, or until the grains are tender but with a slight bite.

2. Add seafood to the risotto and add additional stock, if needed, to make a loose mixture. Cook and stir gently for 3–4 minutes, or until seafood is just cooked. Add pine mushrooms (if used), parsley, spinach and Parmesan. Season well with salt and pepper and toss well to mix and wilt greens, about 1–2 minutes. Transfer to a serving platter or bowl and garnish with green onions, Parmesan cheese and freshly ground black pepper.

> You can make the risotto ahead of time. Stop cooking the rice just before adding the seafood (when the rice still has a little bite). Spread the rice onto a baking sheet and allow to cool. To continue, heat a little stock in a pot and add the rice. Keep adding stock until the rice is soft, then add seafood, continuing on with the recipe. ⑥

Trout Rolls Stuffed with Morel-Potato Mousse

Serves 4

This is a slightly complex dish, but the dramatic presentation and harmonious flavours are worth the extra effort. If the task of de-boning a trout seems daunting, you can sometimes buy trout fillets, or you can ask a good fish seller to prepare the fish for you. Healthy, fresh trout has a natural covering of slime; don't be put off if your fish has a slippery coating. Blanch the leeks (or green onions) by dipping quickly in boiling water; this makes them pliable enough to tightly wrap the fish.

Oven: 350°F / 180°C

Mousse

1 tbsp	olive oil (or butter)	15 mL
1 cup	fresh morels, sliced	250 mL
	(chanterelle, porcini, oyster, button)	
2	medium shallots, diced	2
1 tsp	garlic, minced	5 mL
1 cup	cold mashed potatoes	250 mL
2	eggs, separated	2
2 tbsp	fresh chives, minced	30 mL
	salt and pepper to taste	

Trout

4	fresh trout (1 lb / 450 g each)	4
	(de-boned and cut into fillets, skin off)	
8	leeks (or green onions)	8
	cut in strips, blanched	
2 tbsp	olive oil	30 mL

Sauce

1 cup	dry white wine	250 mL
2 tbsp	whipping cream	30 mL
2 tbsp	chilled butter	30 mL
2 tbsp	fresh chives, minced	30 mL
	additional chives for garnish	

1. In a non-stick skillet, heat oil over high for 45 seconds. Add morels, shallots and garlic. Season well with salt and pepper and sauté until mushrooms begin to brown, about 5 minutes. Allow to cool to handling temperature and reserve.

2. In a medium bowl, combine cooled mushrooms and mashed potatoes. Mix in egg yolks and season well with chives, salt and pepper. In the bowl of a mixer, beat egg whites until very soft peaks are formed. Fold into the potato mixture and chill in the refrigerator for at least 15 minutes.

3. On a flat work surface, place 4 fillets of trout, skinned-side down. Season with salt and pepper and spread mousse on top of each fillet (½ in / 1.2 cm thick). Starting with the tail, roll fillet into a compact bundle. Place a strip of leek or green onion around the roll and tie with a simple knot. Repeat with remaining trout and mousse. Place on a plate and refrigerate until needed.

4. In a non-stick skillet, heat oil over high for 30 seconds. Add trout rolls and fry until browned, about 2–3 minutes per side. Remove from pan, place on parchment-lined baking tray and bake for 7–8 minutes.

5. Meanwhile, return skillet to medium heat, add wine and reduce until 2 tbsp / 30 mL of liquid remains. Add cream, bring to a boil and allow to thicken slightly. Remove from heat and whisk in (or swirl in) the butter until a thick sauce is formed. Add chives, check seasoning and adjust if necessary. To serve, arrange trout rolls on a warm plate with steamed asparagus and new potatoes. Drizzle chive sauce over top and garnish with additional chives.

Baked Portobello Caps Stuffed with Shrimp Cocktail

Serves 4

Portobello caps make a visually stunning presentation. Try to find medium-size caps, 2–3 inches (5–8 cm) in diameter, with a pink or light chocolate blush to the gills. Older mushrooms should be avoided or, if used, the gills should be scraped from inside the cap to give the cleanest flavours.

Oven: 375°F / 190°C

1 cup	shrimp, shelled, de-veined and chopped	250 mL
1/4 cup	ketchup	60 mL
1 tbsp	horseradish	15 mL
1 tsp	hot sauce	5 mL
1 tbsp	fresh basil (or cilantro), chopped	15 mL
4	medium portobello mushrooms (or 16 smaller mushroom caps)	4
1 tbsp	olive oil	15 mL
	salt and pepper to taste	
1/2 cup	Gruyère or Swiss (Emmenthaler) cheese, grated	125 mL

1. In a small bowl, combine shrimp, ketchup, horseradish, hot sauce and basil. Chill until needed.

2. On a parchment-covered baking sheet, place mushroom caps and drizzle with olive oil. Season well with salt and pepper and fill each cap with the shrimp mixture. Top each cap with a spoonful of grated cheese. Place in a hot oven and bake for 5 minutes, or until cheese is melted and beginning to brown. Transfer to a serving platter.

Salmon, Pepper and Mushroom Ragout

Serves 4

Peppers and salmon seem to be a natural combination. Add the peppers near the end of the recipe and cook until just tender. The crunch of the pepper is a nice contrast to the smooth richness of the salmon.

2 tbsp	butter (or olive oil)	30 mL
2 cups	fresh wild mushrooms, sliced	500 mL
	(morel, oyster, cremini, button)	
1 cup	leeks, washed and chopped	250 mL
2 tbsp	garlic, minced	30 mL
	salt and pepper to taste	
1/2 cup	dry white wine	125 mL
2 tbsp	flour	30 mL
2 cups	milk (or stock)	500 mL
2 cups	new potatoes, quartered	500 mL
1	red pepper, seeded and chopped	1
1	yellow pepper, seeded and chopped	1
1 lb	salmon, cubed	450 g
2 tbsp	mixed fresh herbs	30 mL
	(parsley, cilantro, basil, tarragon, and/or chives)	

cont'd on page 172

1. In a large, heavy-bottomed saucepan, add butter and heat over high for 45 seconds. Add mushrooms, leeks and garlic and season well with salt and pepper. Sauté until mushrooms are soft and appear dry, about 5 minutes. Add wine and cook until almost evaporated. Sprinkle flour on top and stir well to mix. Add milk and stir well to dissolve flour and allow mixture to thicken. Add potatoes, reduce heat to low and simmer for 5 minutes.

2. Add peppers and cook for 1–2 minutes. Add salmon and herbs and gently stir the mixture. Simmer for 3–4 minutes or until salmon is just cooked and the potatoes are tender. Season well with salt and pepper and transfer to a serving dish. Serve over mashed potatoes, cooked pasta or rice.

Mussels and Clams in Chardonnay Pine Mushroom Sauce

Serves 4

The spicy flavour of the pine mushrooms melds with the rich, buttery flavour of Chardonnay. If fresh pine mushrooms are not available, chanterelles or shiitakes can be substituted, but the results will pale in comparison. White truffles are a more acceptable alternative.

1 cup	Chardonnay wine	250 mL
2	medium shallots, diced	2
1 tbsp	garlic, minced	15 mL
1 tbsp	fresh thyme, chopped	15 mL
2 lb	clams, washed and scrubbed	1 kg
2 lbs	mussels, washed and scrubbed	1 kg
1 cup	whipping cream	250 mL
1	small pine mushroom, thinly sliced	1
	salt and pepper to taste	
2 cups	spinach, washed, stemmed and chopped	500 mL
1/2	lemon, juice of	1/2

1. In a heavy-bottomed pot, combine the wine, shallots, garlic and thyme. Bring to a boil and add the clams. Cover with a tight-fitting lid and cook for 2–3 minutes. Add the mussels and stir to mix. Continue to cook until all the shells open (large shells take longer to cook through). With a slotted spoon, remove the opened shellfish and transfer to large bowl.

2. Discard any shells that have not opened after 5 minutes of direct heat. Bring the broth to a boil and add the cream and pine mushrooms. Reduce heat to medium and boil until the cream mixture begins to thicken. Check seasoning and adjust with salt and pepper. Add the spinach and lemon juice. Cook until just wilted, pour the sauce over the shellfish and serve warm with a side of French bread.

Smoked Sablefish and Chanterelles Braised in Tomato-Lemon Broth

Serves 4

Sablefish (or black cod) is a rich, oily fish that works with the clean acidity of tomato juice to balance the flavour. Braising renders the chanterelles to a silky and sensual texture. Shiitake mushrooms make a very suitable alternative.

Oven: 350°F / 180°C

1 cup	red wine	250 mL
2 cups	V-8 (or tomato, or Clamato) juice	500 mL
1	lemon, juice and zest	1
½ lb	chanterelles, sliced	225 g
	(shiitake, oyster or cauliflower mushrooms)	
	salt and pepper to taste	
1 ½ lb	natural smoked sablefish in fillets	675 g
	(or haddock)	
1 tbsp	butter	15 mL
2 tbsp	fresh parsley, chopped	30 mL
2 cups	mixed greens, washed and chopped	500 mL
	(spinach, arugula, kale, mustard greens, etc.)	

1. In a large oven-proof skillet (or small, deep roasting pan), combine red wine, tomato juice, lemon zest and juice. Season broth with salt and pepper. Bring to a boil, add chanterelles and fish and carefully transfer to the oven. Cook for 10 minutes, or until the fish is soft and just beginning to flake.

2. Remove from oven and return to the stovetop. Remove fish from sauce and keep warm. Add butter, parsley and mixed greens to the sauce. Toss to mix and heat until greens are wilted, about 1–2 minutes. To serve, transfer to a serving platter and top with the sablefish. Serve with mashed potatoes, rice or pasta.

Grilled Portobello and Halibut with Miso-Honey Glaze

Serves 4

Miso seems to work wonders with the delicate taste of halibut. The marinade tends to firm the structure of the fish and makes the sometimes-bland portobello sing with flavour. Cut the mushrooms and fish into equal-size cubes for even cooking and ease of handling on the grill.

Grill: Hot

2 tbsp	miso	30 mL
2 tbsp	honey	30 mL
1 tbsp	ginger, minced	15 mL
1	lime, juice and zest	1
1 tbsp	sweet soy (or teriyaki) sauce	15 mL
1 lb	fresh halibut fillet, cubed	450 g
½ lb	portobello mushrooms, cubed	225 g
	salt and pepper to taste	
16	wooden skewers (soaked in water)	16
1 tbsp	olive (or vegetable oil)	15 mL

1. In a small bowl, combine miso, honey, ginger, lime juice and zest and soy sauce. Add halibut cubes. Set aside to marinate for at least 10 minutes (but not more than 1 hour).

2. Thread a piece of mushroom on a skewer and top with a piece of halibut. Repeat to fill the skewer. Transfer to a platter and repeat with remaining ingredients. Allow to marinate for at least 10 minutes.

3. Shake skewer free of excess marinade, drizzle with olive oil and season with salt and pepper. Transfer skewers to hot grill (shake off excess oil or sauce). Grill until mushrooms are brown and the halibut has turned firm and pure white. Baste occasionally with the reserved marinade. Transfer to a clean platter and serve with rice or noodles.

Meat and Poultry Dishes

Pancetta-Wrapped Quail Stuffed with Truffle Bread Pudding 178

Roast Vietnamese Pork Rolls with Spinach and Mushrooms 180

Mushroom Diablo Chicken 182

Boneless Lamb Leg with Wild Mushroom Stuffing 183

Braised Duck and Chanterelles in Red Wine-
Blackberry Sauce 185

Osso Bucco with Morels and Baby Leeks 187

Rabbit Fricassee with Horn of Plenty Mushrooms 189

Mushroom-Crusted Prime Rib Roast with Porcini Gravy 191

Pancetta-Wrapped Quail Stuffed with Truffle Bread Pudding

Serves 4–8

Quail is delicately flavoured poultry that should remain tender and juicy when cooked properly. If truffles are not part of your budget, the stuffing is excellent made with dried boletes or horn of plenty mushrooms. Soak mushrooms in boiling water, drain and chop into a fine dice before proceeding. Serve one quail as a delicious appetizer with a salad of mixed greens, Parmesan and sliced pear.

Oven: 375°F / 190°C

Quail

1 cup	cream (or milk)	250 mL
2	eggs	2
1 tsp	truffle (black or white), minced	5 mL
1 tsp	white truffle oil	5 mL
1 tsp	fresh rosemary, minced	5 mL
1 tsp	garlic, minced	5 mL
	salt and pepper to taste	
2 cups	stale French bread, cubed	500 mL
8	quail, de-boned (sleeved)	8
1 tbsp	olive oil	15 mL
8 slices	pancetta (or smoked) bacon	8 slices

Sauce

2 cups	chicken stock	500 mL
2 tbsp	port	30 mL
2 tbsp	chilled butter, cut in small cubes	30 mL

1. In a large bowl, whisk together cream, eggs, truffles, truffle oil, rosemary and garlic. Season well with salt and pepper and fold in bread cubes. Set aside until needed. Add more bread if there is excess liquid in the bowl after 5 minutes of soaking.

2. On a flat work surface, place the quail and rub evenly with olive oil. Season well, inside and out, with salt and pepper. Stuff each de-boned quail with the bread stuffing. Wrap quail with a slice of pancetta and secure with a toothpick or skewer. Fold wing tips under arm to make a compact bundle. Repeat with the remaining quail.

3. In a heavy-bottom roasting pan (or Dutch oven) over medium-high heat, add the oil and heat for 45 seconds. Add the quail and lightly brown on all sides. Transfer to the oven and roast for 15 minutes, or until the bacon is crisp and the quail are cooked through (to an internal temperature of 165°F / 75°C). A metal skewer inserted into the stuffing will be hot to the touch. Allow quail to rest for 10 minutes.

4. In a small saucepan, add the stock and port. Cook until reduced to half the volume. Remove from heat and whisk in the chilled butter. Season with salt and pepper and set aside until glossy. To serve, divide sauce among 4 plates. Cut quail into thick slices and place on top of sauce. Serve with mashed potatoes and sautéed vegetables.

Roast Vietnamese Pork Rolls with Spinach and Mushrooms

Serves 4

Use pork steaks that are marbled with a little fat for best results. The sweet and spicy glaze will burn if left unattended for too long. Keep an eye on the rolls and baste periodically with the glaze to build up a nice finish and leave the pork with a crispy and slightly charred exterior.

Oven: 375°F / 180°C

Vietnamese Glaze

½ cup	mint jelly	125 mL
1 tbsp	hot sauce	15 mL
1 tbsp	chili sauce	15 mL
1 tbsp	garlic, minced	15 mL
1 tbsp	ginger, minced	15 mL
2	limes, zest and juice of	2
1 tbsp	basil, minced	15 mL

Pork Roll

2 lb	4 boneless pork shoulder or butt steaks	1 kg
½ cup	dry white wine	125 mL
1 tbsp	garlic, sliced	15 mL
	salt and pepper to taste	
1 tbsp	olive oil	15 mL
½ lb	mushrooms, sliced	225 g
	(white or brown button, shiitake, portobello)	
½ lb	spinach, washed and stemmed	225 g

1. In a small saucepan, combine mint jelly, hot sauce, chili sauce, garlic, ginger, lime zest and juice and basil. Warm over medium heat, stirring constantly until jelly is dissolved. Set aside until needed.

2. On a cutting board, lay 1 pork steak on a sheet of plastic wrap. Cover with a second sheet and flatten the meat with a tenderizer (or flat blunt instrument). Repeat with remaining pork and transfer to a casserole dish. Add wine and garlic and turn to coat. Set aside to marinate for at least 20 minutes.

3. In a non-stick skillet over medium-high heat, add oil and heat for 45 seconds. Add mushrooms and season well with salt and pepper. Sauté until mushrooms appear dry, about 5 minutes. Add spinach and toss until wilted. Allow to cool and set aside.

4. On a cutting board, place the drained pork. Brush surface with the mint sauce and mound 1/4 of the mushroom mixture in the centre. Roll into a cylinder and tie with butcher's twine into a compact roll. Repeat with remaining rolls.

5. In an oven-proof skillet over medium-high heat, add oil and heat for 1 minute. Add the pork rolls and brown on all sides, about 2–3 minutes per side. Place in oven and baste repeatedly with glaze until the rolls are cooked through (to an internal temperature of 160°F / 71°C) and slightly charred, about 10 minutes. Remove from oven and allow to rest for 10 minutes before cutting the string and carving into slices. Serve with a drizzle of the remaining glaze.

Mushroom Diablo Chicken

Serves 4

Mushrooms contain natural salts and sugars that transform the skin of chicken into a crispy, succulent treat. The lemon juice helps to dry out the skin and adds a tangy flavour. Watch that the skin does not brown too quickly; if it is darkening after 30 minutes, turn down the temperature a few degrees and continue with the roasting.

Oven: 400°F / 200°C

3 lb	roasting chicken	1.35 kg
	salt and pepper to taste	
2 tbsp	garlic, minced	30 mL
1 tsp	hot sauce	5 mL
1 tbsp	ground wild mushroom powder (page 57)	15 mL
1 tbsp	fresh rosemary (or sage), minced	15 mL
1 tsp	paprika (or chili powder)	5 mL
1 tbsp	olive oil	15 mL
1	lemon, juice of	1

1. On a flat work surface, lay the chicken breast-side down. With a sharp knife (or kitchen scissors) cut along the back of the chicken, into the cavity. Pull the sides of the chicken apart and lay skin-side-up on the work surface. Flatten breast with your hands to crack the breast bone. The chicken should lie flat.

2. In a heavy roasting pan, add chicken and season inside and out with salt and pepper. Place bird cavity-side-down in the pan. In a small bowl combine garlic, hot sauce, mushroom powder, rosemary, paprika, oil and lemon juice. Rub chicken with mixture to evenly coat the skin. Allow to marinate for at least 10 minutes.

3. Place in hot oven and roast until skin is crisp and golden brown (to an internal temperature of 165°F / 75°C), about 1 hour. Allow to rest for at least 10 minutes before serving.

Boneless Lamb Leg with Wild Mushroom Stuffing

Serves 4

If the process of de-boning a lamb leg seems daunting to you, ask your local butcher to do the job for you. Have the butcher butterfly the meat to allow you plenty of room for stuffing. The lamb is excellent served with mint or cranberry sauce.

Oven: 375°F / 190°C

Stuffing

1 tbsp	olive oil	15 mL
½ lb	wild mushrooms, sliced	225 g
	(chanterelle, porcini, oyster and morel)	
1	medium onion, diced	1
1 tbsp	garlic, minced	15 mL
	salt and pepper to taste	
1 tbsp	fresh sage, minced	15 mL
1 tbsp	fresh rosemary, minced	15 ml
2 cups	stale bread, cubed	500 mL
1 cup	cold mashed potatoes	250 mL
1	egg, whisked	1

Lamb

4 lb	lamb leg, de-boned	1.8 kg
8	garlic cloves, halved	8
2 tbsp	olive oil	30 mL

cont'd on page 184

1. In a non-stick skillet, heat oil over high heat for 45 seconds. Add mushrooms, onions and garlic and season with salt and pepper. Sauté until mushrooms appear dry, about 5 minutes. Allow to cool to handling temperature. In a large bowl, combine mushroom mixture, sage, rosemary, bread, potatoes and egg. Season with salt and pepper.

2. On a cutting board, place lamb and season well with salt and pepper. Place stuffing in the centre of the lamb. Pull up sides and wrap the meat around the stuffing. Using butcher's twine, tie the lamb into a firm bundle. With a sharp knife, make small cuts in the surface of the lamb and insert garlic into the cuts.

3. Place in a heavy roasting pan, rub surface with olive oil and season with salt and pepper and roast until the skin is crisp and the lamb is cooked through (to an internal temperature of 145°F / 63°C for rare, 160°F / 71°C for medium and 170°F / 77°C for well done). The roast should cook for at least 2 hours. Remove from oven and allow to rest for at least 10 minutes before carving.

On a cutting board, place the leg of lamb and run a sharp knife down the centre of the meat. Cut down to the bone and carefully slice meat until the bone is exposed. The skin will be very tough at the small (shank) end. Slowly run knife along the bone until it can be pulled free of the meat. Lay the lamb skin-side-down on the cutting board, cutting into larger pieces of meat to allow the leg to lie flat.

Braised Duck and Chanterelles in Red Wine-Blackberry Sauce

Serves 4

In this dish, the duck is first pan-fried, allowing you to remove excess quantities of fat from the pan before proceeding with the recipe. Once the dish has cooked and is resting out of the oven, you have a second chance to spoon away unwanted fat. The richness of the dish is wonderful when paired with a full-bodied wine like a Zinfandel or Merlot.

Oven: 325°F / 165°C

1 tbsp	olive oil	15 mL
1 tbsp	ginger, minced	15 mL
1	medium duck (2 lb / 1kg), cut in pieces	1
	salt and pepper to taste	
1 cup	whole shallots, peeled	250 mL
½ lb	chanterelles	225 g
2 tbsp	all-purpose flour	30 mL
2 cups	red wine (Zinfandel or Merlot)	500 mL
2 cups	duck or chicken stock	500 mL
1 cup	fresh or frozen blackberries	250 mL
	(or 2 large spoonfuls of blackberry jam)	

cont'd on page 186

1. In a heavy-bottom roasting pan (or Dutch oven), heat oil over medium-high heat for 1 minute. Add ginger and duck pieces, season well with salt and pepper. Fry until the pieces begin to brown, about 3–4 minutes per side. Remove duck to a plate and set aside. Pour off excess fat (leaving 2 tbsp / 30 mL) and add shallots and chanterelles. Cook until mushrooms are browned, about 5 minutes.

2. Sprinkle pan with flour, stirring well. Return to heat and cook until the mixture starts to brown and stick, about 5 minutes. Add wine, stock and blackberries. Bring to a boil and return duck to the sauce. Cover (with aluminum foil or lid), transfer to the oven and bake for 1 hour or until the duck is tender and falling off the bones.

3. Remove duck from the oven and allow to rest for 5 minutes. Transfer to a serving dish and serve immediately with mashed potatoes and steamed vegetables.

Osso Bucco with Morels and Baby Leeks

Serves 4

Osso bucco is delicious when made with fresh veal or lamb shanks. I've even tried it made with venison (just be careful to remove the sharp tendon bones!). Shanks have lots of natural gelatin and the dish really benefits from being made in advance. As the shanks cook, the natural gelatin dissolves, leaving a rich, soft and flavourful meat. The sauce should solidify into a solid mass when cold. If you are using dried morsels, soak in water for 30 minutes to reconstitute.

Oven: 350°F / 180°C

1 tbsp	olive oil	15 mL
2 lb	veal (or lamb) shanks	1 kg
	(cut in 1 in / 2.5 cm slices)	
	salt and pepper to taste	
1 cup	onion, diced	250 mL
1 cup	carrots, peeled and chopped	250 mL
1 cup	celery, chopped	250 mL
1 cup	white wine	250 mL
20	fresh morels, halved (or dried)	20
16	whole baby leeks, washed	16
	(or 4 larger leeks, quartered)	
8 cups	beef or lamb stock (or water)	2 L

cont'd on page 188

1. In a heavy-bottom roasting pan (or Dutch oven), heat oil over medium-high heat for 1 minute. Add shanks and season with salt and pepper. Turn shanks until all sides are well browned. Remove shanks and transfer to a plate. Stirring constantly, add onions, carrots and celery and season with salt and pepper.

2. Add wine and scrape bottom with a wooden spoon to lift most of the vegetables. Add stock, morels and leeks and bring to a boil. Remove from heat, add shanks, cover (with aluminum foil or lid) and transfer to oven.

3. Braise until meat is tender, about 2 hours. Serve immediately or, for best results, allow shanks to cool to room temperature and re-heat (may be done one day in advance). To serve, warm shanks and sauce over medium heat until warmed through, about 5 minutes. Turn occasionally to distribute the heat. Adjust seasoning with salt and pepper and accompany with mashed potatoes (or polenta) and vegetables.

Rabbit Fricassee with Horn of Plenty Mushrooms

Serves 4

Rabbit is braised in a luscious broth of vegetables, herbs and mushrooms. Be careful not to overcook the rabbit, as the flesh is lean and has a tendency to dry out and become stringy. If left too long in the oven, the meat will break down completely. The horn of plenty is commonly called the "Poor Man's Truffle" and adds a wonderful flavour.

Oven: 350°F / 180°C

2 lb	fresh rabbit	1 kg
1/4 cup	flour (or potato starch)	60 mL
	salt and pepper to taste	
2 tbsp	butter	30 mL
2 tbsp	brandy (or sherry)	30 mL
6 cups	stock or water	1.5 L
2 cups	potato, diced	500 mL
1 cup	carrot, diced	250 mL
1 cup	onion, diced	250 mL
2 tbsp	fresh marjoram, chopped	30 mL
2 tbsp	fresh thyme, chopped	30 mL
2 tbsp	fresh Italian parsley, chopped	30 mL
1 oz	dried horn of plenty mushrooms (or porcini, soaked in hot water)	30 g

cont'd on page 190

1. On a cutting board, cut rabbit into 2 in / 5 cm pieces, using a heavy knife or cleaver (or ask your butcher to cut rabbit into stewing chunks). Rinse rabbit under cold water to remove all traces of blood, and drain in a colander. Season well with salt and pepper.

2. On a plate, place flour and season well with salt and pepper. Roll rabbit pieces in flour to evenly coat. Place pieces on a plate when floured.

3. In a heavy-bottom roasting pan (or Dutch oven), heat butter over high heat for 1 minute. Add rabbit, reduce heat to medium-high, season with salt and pepper and cook rabbit until browned on both sides, about 7–8 minutes. Remove from heat and set aside on a plate. Add stock, potatoes, carrots, onions, marjoram, thyme, parsley and mushrooms. When browned, add brandy and scrape pan until the liquid is almost evaporated.

4. Cover (with aluminum foil or lid), transfer pan to a hot oven and bake for 1 hour. Remove from heat and allow to cool for 10 minutes. Serve with rice, potatoes or polenta and sautéed vegetables.

Mushroom-Crusted Prime Rib Roast
with Porcini Gravy

Serves 4–6

Prime rib is the ultimate beef dinner. Mushroom powder caramelizes on the roast, making a crusty and delicious coating. For well-aged beef, seek out a reputable butcher. A roast that is well marbled with fat will give very tender results.

Oven: 375°F / 190°C

5 lb	prime rib roast	2.25 kg
8	garlic cloves, cut in half	8
1 tbsp	olive oil	15 mL
	salt and pepper to taste	
1 tbsp	ground mushroom powder (page 57)	15 mL
1 tbsp	minced fresh rosemary	15 mL

Gravy

1 cup	onions, diced	250 mL
1 cup	carrots, peeled and chopped	250 mL
1 cup	celery, chopped	250 mL
2 tbsp	garlic, minced	30 mL
1 tbsp	olive oil	15 mL
2 cups	water (or wine)	500 mL
1/4 cup	flour	60 mL
1 tbsp	sherry	15 mL
2 cups	fresh porcini, diced	500 mL
	(button, portobello, chanterelle, morel)	
8 cups	beef or mushroom stock	2 L

cont'd on page 192

1. In a heavy roasting pan, place the roast. With a sharp knife make tiny cuts in the beef and insert pieces of garlic. Rub beef with olive oil and season well with salt and pepper. Evenly sprinkle mushroom powder and rosemary on the beef, rubbing with the hands to distribute the seasoning. Remove roast to a plate and rest for 5 minutes.

2. Add onions, carrots, celery and garlic to pan and drizzle with olive oil. Season with salt and pepper and toss to coat. Return roast to pan rib-side-down on top of the vegetables. Add water and transfer pan to a hot oven and roast until the surface is well browned and cooked through. The roast will cook for at least 2 hours (to an internal temperature of 145°F / 63°C for rare, 160°F / 71°C for medium and 170°F / 77°C for well done).

3. Remove the pan from oven and transfer beef to a platter, cover with aluminum foil and keep warm. Place pan over 2 stove burners and turn heat to medium. Stir vegetables until liquid has evaporated and the mixture is beginning to stick to the bottom and brown. Remove excess fat, leaving 3 tbsp / 45 mL.

4. Sprinkle flour over pan and stir with a wooden spoon or whisk to mix well. Add sherry and stock, 1 cup / 250 mL at a time, until all the liquid is incorporated or you have a gravy consistency. The gravy will thicken as it simmers. Cook for 5 minutes, strain into a second pot, pressing solids with a wooden spoon to extract all the gravy. Meanwhile, in a non-stick skillet over medium-high heat, add 1 tbsp / 15 mL of reserved fat and mushrooms. Sauté until soft and beginning to brown, about 5 minutes. Add mushrooms to gravy and heat through. Add a little extra stock if the gravy is too thick.

5. To serve, carve roast beef into thick slices and serve with gravy, roast potatoes, vegetables and Yorkshire Pudding (page 118).

Further Information

Author Contact

Bill Jones, Magnetic North Cuisine
Webpage: www.magnorth.bc.ca
E-mail: bill@magnorth.bc.ca

Internet Resources

Earthy Delights: fresh and dried wild
mushrooms, food products
www.earthy.com

Fungi Perfecti: medicinal mushroom
products, mushroom teas, dried
mushrooms
www.fungi.com

Mykoweb: Internet mushroom information
and links page, Canadian and U.S.
mycological societies
www.mykoweb.com

Mycological: fresh and dried
mushrooms
www.mycological.com

Wild West Mushroom Company: fresh and
dried wild mushrooms
www.wildwestmushroom.com

Mycological Societies

Vancouver Mycological Society
Box 181
#101-1001 West Broadway
Vancouver, B.C.
Canada V6H 4E4
Webpage: www.interchange.ubc.ca/leathem/
vms/homepage.htm

Mycological Society of Toronto
2 Deepwood Crescent
North York, ON
Canada M3C 1N8
Webpage: www.myctor.org

Cercle des Mycologues de Montréal
Jardin Botanique de Montréal
4101, rue Sherbrooke est
Montréal, PQ
Canada H1X 2B2
Webpage: www.mycomontreal.qc.ca

North American Mycological Association
(NAMA)
10 Lynn Brook Place
Charleston, WV
U.S.A. 25312
Webpage: www.namyco.org

North American Truffling Society (NATS)
P.O. Box 296
Corvallis, OR
U.S.A. 97339

Recommended Books

Field Guides and Handbooks

Arora, David, *All That the Rain Promises, and More...A Hip Pocket Guide to Western Mushrooms.* Berkeley, Ten Speed Press, 1991.

Arora, David, *Mushrooms Demystified.* Berkeley, Ten Speed Press, 1986.

Gibbons, Euell, *Stalking the Wild Asparagus.* New York, David McKay, 1962.*

Hadeler, Hajo, *Medicinal Mushrooms You Can Grow.* Sechelt, B.C., Cariaga, 1994.

Lincoff, Gary, *The Audubon Society Field Guide to North American Mushrooms.* New York, Alfred A. Knopf, 1981.

McKenny, Margaret, and Daniel E. Stuntz, *The New Savory Wild Mushroom.* Seattle, University of Washington Press, 1987.

McKnight, Kent, and Vera McKnight, *Peterson Flashguide: Mushrooms.* Houston, Houghton Mifflin Company, 1996.

Ratzloff, John, *The Moral Mushroom: A Guide For Roons.* Stillwater, MN, Voyageur, 1990.*

Schalkwijk-Barendsen, Helene M. E., *Mushrooms of Western Canada.* Edmonton, Lone Pine, 1991.

Smith, Alexander, *A Field Guide to Western Mushrooms.* Ann Arbor, University of Michigan Press, 1975.

Turner, Nancy J., *Food Plants of Coastal First Peoples.* Vancouver, UBC Press, 1995.

Turner, Nancy J., *Food Plants of Interior First Peoples,* Vancouver, UBC Press, 1997.

Underhill, J. E., *Guide to Western Mushrooms.* Surrey, B.C., Hancock House, 1996.

Mushroom Cookbooks

Barber, James, *Mushrooms are Marvellous.* Vancouver, Douglas & McIntyre Ltd., 1984.*

Carluccio, Antonio, *A Passion for Mushrooms.* London, Pavilion Books, 1989.*

Czarnecki, Jack, *Joe's Book of Mushroom Cookery.* Toronto, Collier MacMillian of Canada Inc., 1986.

Czarnecki, Jack, *A Cook's Book of Mushrooms.* New York, Artisan, 1995.

Gardon, Anne, ed., *The Wild Food Gourmet.* Toronto, Firefly Books, 1998.

Jordan, Peter, and Stephen Wheeler, *The Ultimate Mushroom Book.* London, Lorenz Books, 1998.*

Style, Sue, *Fruits of the Forest — Cooking with Wild Food.* London, Pavilion Books, 1995.

* out of print

Index

Abalone mushrooms. *See* Oyster mushrooms
Agaricus mushrooms. *See* Button mushrooms
Aïoli, Sherry, 124–25
    See also Mayonnaise, Ginger
Amanita mushrooms, 19, 21, 42, 44, 45
Angel wings, 42
APPETIZERS
    Chanterelle, Caramelized Onion and Asiago
        Quesadillas, 77–78
    Dungeness Crab and Enoki Mushroom Cakes,
        75–76
    Grilled Oyster Mushroom Skewers, 68
    Mushroom, Ham and Swiss Cheese Nachos, 79
    Mushroom and Shrimp Gyoza, 69–70
    Pancetta-Wrapped Quail Stuffed with Truffle
        Bread Pudding, 178–79
    Pan-fried Tuna and Mushroom Bundles, 80–81
    Phyllo Spring Rolls Stuffed with Mushrooms
        and Vegetables, 71–72
    Portobello and Green Onion Pancakes with
        Plum Sauce, 146–47
    Wild Mushroom and Goat Cheese Pâté, 73–74
    Wine-Pickled Mushrooms, 65
Asparagus, 85, 110–11, 156–57

Bacon, 104–5, 178–79
Barley, pearl, 96–97, 108–9, 129, 154–55
Bean sprouts, 71–72, 94–95, 112–13, 138–39, 140–41
Blackberries, 185–86
Black mushrooms. *See* Shiitake(s)
Bok choy, baby, 88, 142–43
Boletes, 3, 15, 22, 24, 25
    about, 32–35
    dried, in Bread Pudding, 178
    See also Cèpes; Porcini
Broccoli, 161
Broths, 94–95, 96–97
    See also Stocks
Button mushrooms, 10, 24, 25
    about, 45
        brown, 50 (*see also* Cremini)
        white, 2, 22, 26, 49–50
    in Crispy Potato-Onion Pancakes, 159–60
    in Mushroom Corn Sauce, 148–49
    in Smoked Cod and Mushroom Potato Cakes,
        124–25

Cabbage, 71–72, 140–41, 146–47
    and Mushroom Coleslaw, 103
    Rolls, with Chanterelles, 154–55
    See also Sui choy
Cardamom, 92, 93
Carrots, 103, 108–9
Cauliflower, 84, 161
Cauliflower fungi, 4, 22, 23, 24, 25
    about, 43
    in Purée of Leeks, with Cardamom, 92–93
Cèpes, 32
    about, 33–34
    in French Onion and Cèpe Soup, 86–87
    See also Boletes; Porcini
Chanterelle(s), 4, 14–15, 22, 24, 25, 26
    about, 29–32
    and Aged Cheddar Frittata, 150–51
    Bacon-Roasted, in Caesar Salad, 104–5
    and Braised Duck, 185–86
    Caramelized Onion and Asiago Quesadillas,
        77–78
    and Cauliflower Chowder, 84
    Leek and Cheddar Polenta, 116
    and Smoked Black Cod, 174
    and Spiced Turkey over Egg Noodles, 142–43
CHEESE
    Asiago, 77–78, 117, 150–51, 156–57
    Cheddar, 77–78, 116, 117, 150–51
    goat, 73–74, 126–27
    Gruyère, 77–78, 86–87, 122–23, 170
    Mozzarella, 132–33
    Parmesan, 126–27, 134, 148–49, 166–67
    ricotta, 132–33
    Swiss, 79, 170
Chicken mushrooms, 22, 44
Chinese mushrooms. *See* Shiitake(s)
Cod, smoked black, 124–25, 174
Corn, 117, 137, 148–49
Cornbread, Mushroom and Herb, 117
Cornmeal, 116, 117, 124–25, 148–49
Cortinarius mushrooms, 43
Cremini, 22, 26, 50
Croutons, Gruyère, 86
Cucumber, 102

Dried mushrooms, 24, 31, 33, 35, 42, 56
    in Asparagus Cream Soup with Sautéed Morels,
        85
    in Mushroom Ginger Tea, 61
    in Mushroom Powder, 57
    in Mushroom Stocks, 59, 60
    in Scalloped Potatoes and Mushrooms, 122–23
    and substitution for fresh, 10–11
    See also names of mushrooms
Dumplings, 69–70

Eggs and mushrooms, 41, 150–51
Enoki mushrooms, 9, 22
    about, 50–51
    in Dungeness Crab Cakes, 75–76

Fairy ring mushrooms, 44
Fennel, 90–91
Field mushrooms. *See* Button mushrooms
FISH
    Halibut, Grilled, and Portobello, 175
    Salmon, Pepper and Mushroom Ragout, 171–72
    Trout Rolls Stuffed with Morel-Potato Mousse,
        168–69
    Tuna and Mushroom Bundles, 80–81
    white, in Dungeness Crab and Enoki Mushroom
        Cakes, 75–76
    See also Cod, smoked black; Seafood

Garlic, 128, 183–84, 191–92
Ginger, 61, 65, 110–11
    Mayonnaise, 75–76, 80
Girolles, 30
    See also Chanterelles
Glazes, 175, 180–81
Golden needle mushrooms. *See* Enoki mushrooms
Gravy, 60, 159–60, 191–92
Greens, 106–7, 174
    See also Cabbage; Lettuce; Spinach
Grilling of mushrooms, 25, 68, 106–7
Gyoza, Mushroom and Shrimp, 69–70

Haddock, 174
Ham, 79, 129
    See also Bacon
Hedgehog mushrooms, 4, 22, 24, 25, 45
Honey mushrooms, 45
Horn of plenty mushrooms, 22, 24, 25, 32
    dried, 178, 189–90
Host mushrooms, 13, 46

Kale, 90–91, 174

Lactarius mushrooms, 44, 46
Lamb, 96–97, 183–84, 187–88
Lawyer's wig mushrooms. *See* Shaggy mane
    mushrooms
Leek(s), 71–72, 108–9, 154–55, 156–57, 168–69,
    171–72
    Baby, with Morels in Osso Bucco, 187–88
    Chanterelle and Cheddar Polenta, 116
    Purée, with Oyster Mushrooms and Cardamom,
        92–93
    Wild Mushroom, Goat Cheese and Walnut
        Risotto, 126–27
Lepiota mushrooms, 47
Lettuce, 71–72, 104–5
Lobster mushrooms, 13, 22, 46

Mayonnaise, Ginger, 75–76, 80
    See also Aïoli, Sherry
MEAT DISHES
    Boneless Lamb Leg with Wild Mushroom
        Stuffing, 183–84
    Mushroom-Crusted Prime Rib Roast with
        Porcini Gravy, 191–92
    Osso Bucco with Morels and Baby Leeks,
        187–88
    Rabbit Fricassee with Horn of Plenty
        Mushrooms, 189–90
    Roast Vietnamese Pork Rolls with Spinach and
        Mushrooms, 180–81
    Spaghetti with Mushroom-Beef Balls, 135–36
    See also Bacon; Ham
Miso, 60, 175
Morel(s), 22, 24
    about, 35–37
    and Baby Leeks, in Osso Bucco, 187–88
    in Japanese Rice Salad, with Asparagus, 110–11
    New Potato, Asparagus and Asiago Gratin,
        156–57
    -Potato Mousse, Trout Rolls Stuffed with,
        168–69
    Sautéed, in Asparagus Cream Soup, 85
Mushroom foraging, 2–3, 8, 15–18, 40–41, 46
    field guides, 11, 19, 195
    on the Northwest Coast, 12–15, 29–30, 31
    commercial, 11, 42
    See also Mushrooms, wild
Mushroom poisoning, 18–21
    See also Mushrooms, poisonous

Mushroom Powder, 57
Mushroom recipes
  basic, 55–65
  best for freezing, 58, 62, 69, 132, 135–36
  to make ahead, 69, 96–97, 108–9, 167
  and substitution, 9–10, 11, 26–27
Mushrooms
  about, 7–8
  and alcohol, 17, 36, 47
  benefits of, 7, 9, 53
  cooking with, 2–3, 26, 195
  in Europe/Asia, 2–4, 9, 30, 41, 42, 44, 53
  and pollution, 9, 44
  preparation of, 17, 23
  sources of, 10
  types of, 10, 29–47, 49–53
Mushrooms, cultivated, 49–53
  See also names of mushrooms
Mushrooms, dried. *See* Dried mushrooms
Mushrooms, medicinal, 7, 9, 61
Mushrooms, poisonous, 1, 2, 10, 34–35
  See also Mushroom poisoning; Poisonous
    look-alikes
Mushrooms, wild, 29–47
  cooked vs. raw, 17, 21, 36
  handling and storage, 16–17, 21–22, 26
  and identification, 10, 17, 18–19, 56
  See also Mushroom foraging; *names of
    mushrooms*
Mycological societies, 19, 194
  See also Vancouver Mycological Society

Nachos, Mushroom, Ham and Swiss Cheese, 79
NOODLES AND PASTA
  Crispy Chow Mein Cake with Mushroom and
    Wine Sauce, 138–39
  Macaroni and Mushroom Salad, 102
  in Mushroom Minestrone, 90–91
  Mushroom, Spinach and Ricotta Lasagna,
    132–33
  Rice Noodles with Shiitake, Corn and Oyster
    Sauce, 137
  Shanghai Noodles with Shredded Mushrooms
    and Vegetables, 140–41
  Shiitake Mushroom and Rice Noodle Salad,
    112–13
  Spaghetti with Mushroom-Beef Balls, 135–36
  Spaghettini with Mushrooms, Shallots and
    Garlic, 134

Spiced Turkey and Mushrooms over Egg Noodles,
    142–43

Onion, 77–78, 86–87, 100–101, 159–60
  green, 146–47
Osso Bucco with Morels and Baby Leeks, 187–88
Oyster mushrooms, 9, 22, 24
  about, 46, 51
  Grilled, 68, 106–7, 152–53
  in Purée of Leeks, with Cardamom, 92–93
  Sautéed, and Pea Tops, 158
  in Wild Mushroom and Goat Cheese Pâté,
    73–74
Oyster sauce, 137

Pancakes, 146–47, 159–60
Pasta. *See* Noodles and Pasta
Pâté, Wild Mushroom and Goat Cheese, 73–74
Peanuts, 152–53
Peppers, 79, 152–53, 171–72
Pine mushroom(s), 22, 24, 25, 26, 31
  about, 41–42
  Chardonnay Sauce for Mussels and Clams, 173
  in Mashed Potatoes with Mushrooms and
    Garlic, 120–21
  in Mushroom Broth, with Barbecued Duck
    Wontons, 94-95
  in Mushroom and Seafood Risotto, 166–67
  in Scalloped Potatoes and Mushrooms, 122–23
Poisonous look-alikes, 19, 42, 43, 44–45, 47
  See also Mushrooms, poisonous
Polenta, 116, 148–49
Pom pom (bear's paw), 22
Porcini mushrooms, 22, 26
  Gravy, for Mushroom-Crusted Prime Rib Roast,
    191–92
  sautéed, in Warm Salad of Porcini and Barley,
    108–9
  See also Boletes; Cèpes
Portobellini mushrooms, 50
Portobello mushrooms, 22, 26
  about, 50
  Baked, Stuffed with Shrimp Cocktail, 170
  and Green Onion Pancakes, 146–47
  Grilled, and Halibut with Miso-Honey Glaze,
    175
  julienned, 147
  in Spiced Turkey and Mushrooms over Egg
    Noodles, 142–43

Potato(es), 57, 84, 108–9, 189–90
  in Crispy Potato-Onion Pancakes, 159–60
  flour/starch, 159–60, 189–90
  mashed, 120–21, 124–25, 168–69, 183–84
  new, 156–57, 171–72
  Scalloped, and Mushrooms, 122–23
POULTRY DISHES
  Barbecued Duck Wontons in Mushroom Broth,
    94–95
  Braised Duck and Chanterelles in Red
    Wine–Blackberry Sauce, 185–86
  Mushroom Diablo Chicken, 182
  Pancetta-Wrapped Quail Stuffed with Truffle
    Bread Pudding, 178–79
  Spiced Turkey and Mushrooms over Egg
    Noodles, 142–43
Preserving mushrooms, 21–26
  drying, 24, 26 (*see also* Dried mushrooms)
  freezing, 25–26, 34
  pickling, 65
Puffballs, 47

Rice, 110–11, 126–27, 128, 154–55, 166–67
Rice noodles, 112–13, 137
Risotto, 126–27, 166–67
Ruffle mushrooms. *See* Cauliflower fungi
Russula mushrooms, 13, 46

Saffron milk cap, 25
Salad dressings, 102, 104–5, 110–11
  See also Mayonnaise, Ginger; Vinaigrettes
SALADS
  Caesar Salad with Bacon-Roasted Chanterelles,
    104–5
  Grilled Oyster Mushrooms on Mixed Greens,
    106–7
  Japanese Rice Salad with Morels and Asparagus,
    110–11
  Macaroni and Mushroom Salad with Creamy
    Cucumber Dressing, 102
  Mushroom and Cabbage Coleslaw, 103–4
  Shiitake Mushroom and Rice Noodle Salad,
    112–13
  Spinach Salad with Mushrooms and Roasted
    Onions, 100–101
  Warm Salad of Porcini and Barley, 108–9
SAUCES
  Black Bean, 161
  Chardonnay Pine Mushroom, 173
  chive, for Stuffed Trout Rolls, 169

  Dipping, 69–70, 71, 80
  Mushroom Corn, 148–49
  Mushroom Powder for, 57
  Mushroom Stocks for, 58–60
  Mushroom-Tomato, 62, 132–33, 135–36
  Mushroom and Wine, 138–39
  for Pancetta-Wrapped Quail, 178–79
  Peanut Curry, 152–53
  Plum, 146–47
  Shiitake, Corn and Oyster, 137
  for Shiitake Mushrooms and Scallops, 164–65
  Star Anise Tomato, 154–55
  See also Gravy
Sautéing of mushrooms, 17, 25, 34, 63
SEAFOOD
  Baked Portobello Caps Stuffed with Shrimp
    Cocktail, 170
  Dungeness Crab and Enoki Mushroom Cakes,
    75–76
  Hot and Sour Mushroom Prawn Soup, 88
  Mushroom and Seafood Risotto, 166–67
  Mushroom and Shrimp Gyoza, 69–70
  Mussels and Clams in Chardonnay Pine
    Mushroom Sauce, 173
  Pan-fried Shiitake Mushrooms and Scallops in
    Rice Paper, 164–65
  See also Fish
Shaggy mane mushrooms, 9, 16, 46–47
Shiitake(s), 9, 22
  about, 51–52
  dried, 11, 60, 61
  in Hot and Sour Mushroom Prawn Soup, 88–89
  -Miso Stock (or gravy), 60
  in Mushroom and Shrimp Gyoza, 69–70
  in Pan-fried Tuna and Mushroom Bundles,
    80–81
  in Rice Noodles with Shiitake, Corn and Oyster
    Sauce, 137
  and Scallops in Rice Paper, Pan-fried, 164–65
  with Smoked Black Cod Braised in Tomato-
    Lemon Broth, 174
  Soy-Marinated, in Rice Noodle Salad, 112–13
SIDE DISHES
  Chanterelle, Leek and Cheddar Polenta, 116
  Mashed Potatoes with Mushrooms and Garlic,
    120–21
  Mushroom and Herb Cornbread, 117
  Mushroom, Prosciutto and Barley Pilaf, 129
  Mushroom Yorkshire Pudding, 118–19
  Sautéed Mushrooms, 63

Scalloped Potatoes and Mushrooms, 122–23
Smoked Cod and Mushroom Potato Cakes,
  124–25
Steamed Mushrooms with Garlic-Herb Butter,
  64
Steamed Rice with Wild Mushrooms and Garlic,
  128
Wild Mushroom, Leek, Goat Cheese and Walnut
  Risotto, 126–27
Wine-Pickled Mushrooms, 65
Silver ear fungi. *See* White cloud fungi
Snow peas, 88, 161
SOUPS
  Asparagus Cream, with Sautéed Morels, 85
  Chanterelle and Cauliflower Chowder, 84
  dessert, white cloud fungus in, 53
  French Onion and Cèpe, with Gruyère
    Croutons, 86–87
  Hot and Sour Mushroom Prawn, 88–89
  Mushroom Minestrone, 90–91
  Purée of Leeks, Oyster Mushrooms and
    Cardamom, 92–93
  See also Broths; Stocks, Mushroom
Spinach, 158, 166–67, 173, 174, 180–81
  in Mushroom, Spinach and Ricotta Lasagna,
    132–33
  Salad with Mushrooms and Sweet Roasted
    Onions, 100–101
Spring Rolls, Phyllo, Stuffed with Mushrooms and
  Vegetables, 71–72
Stocks, Mushroom
  Basic, 58
  Instant, 59
  Shiitake-Miso, 60
Storage of mushrooms, 16–17, 23, 26
Straw mushrooms, 22, 52
Stuffings, 71–72, 168–69, 170, 178–79, 183–84
Sui choy, 69–70, 138–39, 148–49

Tea, Mushroom Ginger, 61
Tofu, 88, 94
Tomato(es), 62, 79, 174
Tree ear fungi. *See* Wood ear fungi
Truffle(s), 3–4, 22, 26–27, 116, 173
  about, 38–42
  Bread Pudding, for Pancetta-Wrapped Quail,
    178–79
  in Mashed Potatoes with Mushrooms and
    Garlic, 120–21
Truffle oil(s), 27, 38, 178–79

Vancouver Mycological Society, 4, 12, 19, 194
VEGETARIAN DISHES
  Chanterelle and Aged Cheddar Frittata, 150–51
  Chanterelle Cabbage Rolls with Star Anise
    Tomato Sauce, 154–55
  Crispy Potato-Onion Pancakes with Mushroom
    Gravy, 159–60
  Grilled Peppers and Mushrooms with Peanut
    Curry Sauce, 152–53
  Morel, New Potato, Asparagus and Asiago
    Gratin, 156–57
  Mushroom Polenta with Spicy Mushroom-Corn
    Sauce, 148–49
  Phyllo Spring Rolls Stuffed with Mushrooms
    and Vegetables, 71–72
  Portobello and Green Onion Pancakes with
    Plum Sauce, 146–47
  Sautéed Oyster Mushrooms and Pea Tops, 158
  Shanghai Noodles with Shredded Mushrooms
    and Vegetables, 140–41
  Stir-fried Vegetables and Mushrooms in Black
    Bean Sauce, 161
  See also Salads; Soups
Vinaigrettes, 106–7, 108–9

Walnuts, 126–27
White cloud fungi, 22, 53
Wine-Pickled Mushrooms, 65
Wontons, 69–70
Wood blewit, 43
Wood ear fungi, 9, 22, 24
  about, 52
  in Hot and Sour Mushroom Prawn Soup, 88

Yellow foot mushrooms, 4, 31
Yellow tooth mushrooms. *See* Hedgehog mush-
  rooms
Yorkshire Pudding, Mushroom, 118–19